# THE CAN'T COOK BOOK

## 100+ RECIPES FOR THE ABSOLUTELY TERRIFIED!

ALSO BY JESSICA SEINFELD

**Deceptively Delicious!**
Simple Secrets to Get Your Kids Eating Good Food

**Double Delicious!**
Good, Simple Food for Busy, Complicated Lives

# THE CAN'T COOK BOOK

## 100+ RECIPES FOR THE ABSOLUTELY TERRIFIED!

### BY JESSICA SEINFELD

Photographs by **JOHN KERNICK** • Cover Photography by **MARK SELIGER**

Design & Illustrations by **3&CO.** • Food Styling by **SARA QUESSENBERRY**

**ATRIA** BOOKS

New York London Toronto Sydney New Delhi

**ATRIA** BOOKS

A Division of Simon & Schuster, Inc.
1230 Avenue of the Americas
New York, NY 10020

First Atria Books hardcover edition September 2013

**ATRIA** BOOKS and colophon are trademarks of Simon & Schuster, Inc.

For information about special discounts for bulk purchases,
please contact Simon & Schuster Special Sales at
1-866-506-1949 or business@simonandschuster.com.

The Simon & Schuster Speakers Bureau can bring authors
to your live event. For more information or to book an event,
contact the Simon & Schuster Speakers Bureau at
1-866-248-3049 or visit our website at www.simonspeakers.com.

Art direction, design, and illustration by 3&Co.
Photographs by John Kernick
Cover photography by Mark Seliger
Food styling by Sara Quessenberry

Manufactured in China

10  9  8  7  6  5  4  3  2

Library of Congress Cataloging-in-Publication Data
Seinfeld, Jessica.
  The can't cook book : recipes for the absolutely terrified! / Jessica Seinfeld.
p.  cm.
1. Cooking. 2. Quick and easy cooking. I. Title.
TX643.S455    2013
641.5'55—dc23    2012039499

ISBN 978-1-4516-6225-2
ISBN 978-1-4516-6632-8 (ebook)

To my husband, my muse

*(and to all the other "Can't Cooks" in the world)*

# Contents

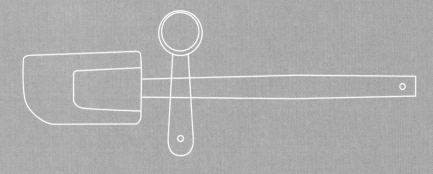

INTRODUCTION FOR CAN'T COOKS...........................1
GEAR UP.................................................... 7
STOCK UP.................................................. 19
SET UP ..................................................... 21
HOW-TO.................................................... 23
RECIPES ................................................... 45
QUICKIES .................................................219
OTHER USEFUL THINGS......................... 228

INDEX ..................................................... 236
ACKNOWLEDGMENTS ............................. 245

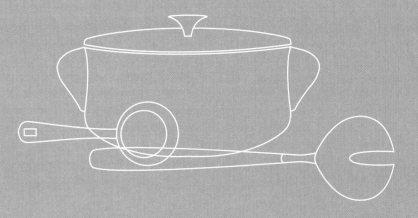

# The Recipes

## BREAKFAST

Scrambled Eggs & Cream Cheese ...................... 47
Fried Eggs over Broiled Tomatoes ...................... 49
Soft-boiled Eggs with Toast ................................ 51
Sweet Pea & Onion Frittata ............................... 53
Huevos Rancheros ............................................. 55
Shepherd's French Toast ................................... 57
Lemon Ricotta Pancakes ................................... 59
Banana-Date Bran Muffins ................................ 61
Fresh Berry Crumb Cake ................................... 63

## CHICKEN

Pan-Roasted Chicken Breasts ............................. 67
Skillet-Roasted Potatoes & Chicken ................... 69
Chicken with Rice & Peas .................................. 71
Rosemary Chicken Under a "Brick" .................... 73
Fast & Juicy Herb-Grilled Chicken ..................... 75
Crispy Chicken Cutlets with Arugula & Lemon ....77
Roasted Chicken, Sweet Potatoes & Tomatoes ...79
Sweet & Spicy Chicken Wings ............................ 81
Roasted Chicken Drumsticks—4 Easy Recipes! ...83
Seriously Basic Roast Chicken ............................ 85

## MEAT

Simple Peppercorn Steak .................................... 89
Herb-Roasted Beef with Potatoes & Carrots ....... 91
Chili-Rubbed Skirt Steak Tacos .......................... 93
The Most Simple, Broiled, Perfect Hamburger ....95
Your First Chili ................................................. 97
Bacon-Wrapped Meat Loaf ................................ 99
Pork Loin with Apples & Onions ...................... 101
Apple Cider Pork Chops ................................... 103
Broiled Lamb Chops with Mint Jelly ................. 105

## FISH

Roasted Striped Bass & Tomatoes ..................... 109
Succulent Lemon-Thyme Salmon ....................... 111
Bread Crumb Bass ............................................ 113
Perfect Halibut over Spinach ............................. 115
Hoisin Halibut ................................................. 117
Crispy Shrimp ................................................. 119
Stewy Shrimp with Tomatoes & White Beans ..... 121

## PASTA & PIZZA

Sweet Cherry Tomato Pasta ............................... 125
Freaky Greek Pasta ........................................... 127
Turkey Bolognese ............................................. 129
Baked Egg Noodles & Cheese ........................... 131
Spaghetti Marinara ........................................... 133
Slow-Cooker Lasagna ....................................... 135
Cacio e Pepe .................................................... 137
Slammin' Pasta with Clams ............................... 139
Pesto Pasta ...................................................... 141
Pizza Margherita .............................................. 143

## VEGETABLES

Broccoli with Golden Raisins & Garlic ............... 147
Green Beans with Almonds ............................... 149
Sautéed Spinach & Garlic ................................. 151
Smashed Red Potatoes with Chives ................... 153
Roasted Asparagus with Lemon ......................... 155
Roasted Eggplant & Cherry Tomatoes ............... 157
Roasted Cauliflower & Sage .............................. 159
Roasted Brussels Sprouts ................................. 161
Oven Fries (carrot, parsnip, russet) ................... 163
Roasted Lemon-Thyme Portobello Mushrooms .165
Roasted Sweet Potato Coins .............................. 167

Minty Sugar Snaps ................................. 169
Summer Tomato Bruschetta ........................ 171
Mexican Corn ...................................... 173
Kale Chips ........................................ 175

## GRAINS & BEANS

Brown Rice Pilaf .................................. 179
Sweet Pea Bulgur Wheat Pilaf ...................... 181
Toasted Pine Nut & Cranberry Quinoa ............... 183
Couscous Salad .................................... 185
Garlic & Rosemary Cannellini Beans ................ 187
Stir-fried Rice with Sunny-side Up Eggs ........... 189

## SALADS

Kale Salads—3 Easy Recipes! ....................... 193
Butter Lettuce Salad with Pine Nuts & Parsley ... 195
Warm Spinach Salad with Blue Cheese ............... 197
Tomato & Watermelon Salad ......................... 199
Chicken Salad with Apples & Basil ................. 201

## DESSERTS

Chocolate Chip Cookies ............................ 205
Oatmeal, Maple & Raisin Cookies ................... 207
Chocolate Chia Drops .............................. 209
Peanut Butter Drops ............................... 209
Cherry-Ginger-Almond Drops ........................ 209
Flourless Fudge Cake with Whipped Cream ...... 211
Broiled Honey-Nut Bananas ......................... 213
Marinated Strawberries with Ice Cream ............. 215
Mixed Berry Crisp ................................. 217

## QUICKIES

Make-It-Yourself Muesli ........................... 220
Cottage Cheese & Pomegranate Seeds ............ 220
English Muffin with Peanut Butter,
    Banana & Coconut .............................. 221
Strawberries with Yogurt & Balsamic .............. 221
Avocado Toast ..................................... 222
Broiled Grapefruit with Almonds & Honey ........ 222
Tomato & Ricotta on Toast ......................... 223
Blueberry-Almond Smoothie ......................... 223
Rice Cake with Cucumbers & Salsa .................. 224
Feta & Bean Flatbread ............................. 224
Apple-Cheddar Melt ................................ 225
Arugula, Dates, Blue Cheese & Almonds .......... 225
Cottage Cheese–Stuffed Avocado ................... 226
Prosciutto, Pear & Parmesan ....................... 226
Tuna & Apple Pita Pizza ........................... 227
Sliced Tomato & Egg Open-Face Sandwich ....... 227

## OTHER USEFUL THINGS

Ruler ............................................. 228
What's in Season? ................................. 229
Meat Temperature Chart ............................ 231
Storage Guidelines & Food Safety Pointers ....... 232
Measurement Conversions & Equivalents .......... 234

For nutritional information on the recipes, go to: **tccb.co**

ix

# INTRODUCTION FOR CAN'T COOKS

Even though I've cooked my whole life, and it's always come quite easily to me, I've had long and intimate relationships with many Can't Cooks.

I live with a Can't Cook, I have family members who are Can't Cooks, and many of my best friends are Can't Cooks. I know who you are, I know what you think, and I know how you feel. I know all the different types of Can't Cooks— The Won't Cooks, The Tried to Cooks, The Hate to Cooks, The Too Busy to Cooks, The Used to Cooks, The Publicly Humiliated Last Time I Cooked Cooks, and "That's the Last Time I Ever Cook for You Ingrates" Cooks.

The thing I've found with Can't Cooks is they almost always grew up in a kitchen where there was a lot of stress around cooking and food. If you never had a person around you in the kitchen who was encouraging, helpful, and clear—I want to be that person for you. You can start fresh here. No judging, no embarrassment, in fact, I'm going to personally guarantee you some fun while you're learning this new skill.

I think one of the biggest reasons people never face cooking is that mistakes along the way are particularly exposed. When you burn something horribly, it's there on the plate for everybody to laugh at. When you fall learning to ice-skate, you can quickly get back up and hopefully nobody even knows it happened.

Remember when you were little, that look on your mother's face when you gave her that mud pie you made? She loved it just because you made it for her. With this book, I guarantee you are going to make things that will taste better than that, but the feeling's going to be the same. You know that feeling when you hit the bull's-eye with that perfect birthday gift for someone you love? Cooking can feel like that.

Most beginner cookbooks do not address the number one problem of the Can't Cook— fear. The idea that a person with no cooking experience can pick up a cookbook and just follow the instructions successfully is a crock. I've heard from so many Can't Cooks who have tried a recipe only to find halfway through there's a tricky technique, some weird foreign words, and some pre-preparation that nobody mentioned. And that's when the panic hits. To avoid all of this, every recipe we're going to do together has clearly defined "Don't Panic" instructions.

This book has more than one hundred photographed recipes, written specifically for people with less than zero experience in a kitchen. If the only cooking you've done is stirring a spoon in a cup of coffee, you will be able to do these. But if you are still feeling worried, the How-to section will show you basic techniques such as chopping garlic and slicing an onion.

To take you a step or two further, there are links to videos of me showing you exactly How-to. You can watch them by logging on to **www.tccb.co** or by scanning the watermarked photos with a free app that you can get at **scannow.mobi/tccb**.

And if that isn't enough, I even have some recipes that require little or no cooking at all—called Quickies. Because sometimes even Can Cooks don't want to cook. (See Tomato & Ricotta on Toast, page 223.)

Even though I believe cooking can be a simple skill, it gives you back so much more. When someone looks up at you after a bite of something you've made and says, "Hey! This is really good!" you'll have a certain kind of inside smile that's like nothing else.

# LOOK AT YOU! YOU'RE HOLDING A COOKBOOK!

Being an adult beginner at anything is unnerving. No one likes to leave his comfort zone. Cooking as a beginner can make you feel very inept, uncomfortable, and even scared. But not for long, my friend. You're already showing some potential. Of course, in any new learning experience, there are setbacks. The fun thing about cooking is that sometimes those setbacks can lead to unintended but surprisingly good results. Believe it or not, cooking can even feel relaxing and spontaneous—but that comes in time, once you are comfortable. Leading up to that point means messing up once in a while. So don't let inevitable mistakes scare you. If you have a dog, he may end up loving this new hobby of yours. **So let's get you up and running.**

One of the first things we're going to undertake is turning your kitchen into a place where you enjoy working. You will learn what everything looks like and what it does. Your kitchen will be stocked with a few simple items

and ingredients you will love using. I will set you up with a starting routine that is exactly the same every time, no matter what you are cooking. You'll feel organized, calm, and ready for anything. This is the essence of being a Can Cook.

In the next few pages, there are lots of photos, along with simple lists of the equipment and ingredients you'll need. This detailed guide will organize you, educate you, and keep your fear at bay. I will help you establish a routine before you even start getting into the recipes. Utilizing certain pots and pans, easily found ingredients, and a consistent setup will make things predictable. Every time you think about cooking something, you will actually know where to begin. The How-to section will break it way down for you with step-by-step photos that will help give you the skills and confidence to jump-start your cooking life. The How-to videos make things crystal clear.

If you are still wondering if you can do this, let me tell you, the recipes that follow have been vetted, debugged, and lab-tested by some of the clumsiest, most useless individuals I've ever met (yes, Jerry, I'm talking about you) and they still worked.

So let's get going. Get the old newspapers and magazines out of the oven, drag that wedding gift pot set out of the basement, clear out that drawer full of takeout menus from the '80s. And fire up the pilot light—we're going in.

# YOU CAN DO THIS.

*Jessica*

Don't these little toys look like fun? You get to use them all throughout this book. Here are some things to keep in mind as you proceed.

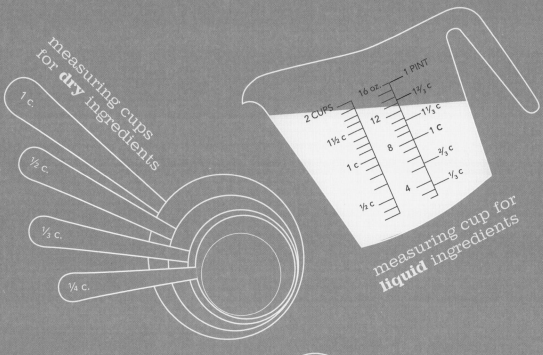

measuring cups for **dry** ingredients

1 c.

½ c.

⅓ c.

¼ c.

2 CUPS
1½ c
1 c
½ c
16 oz.
12
8
4
1 PINT
1⅔ c
1⅓ c
1 c
⅔ c
⅓ c

measuring cup for **liquid** ingredients

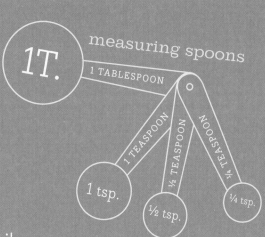

measuring spoons

1T.

1 TABLESPOON

1 TEASPOON

½ TEASPOON

¼ TEASPOON

1 tsp.

½ tsp.

¼ tsp.

**Abbreviations:**

**T.** = tablespoon
**tsp.** = teaspoon
**c.** = cup
**qt.** = quart
**oz.** = ounce
**lb.** = pound
**e.v. olive oil** = extra virgin olive oil

# GEAR UP
## STOCK UP
## SET UP
## How-to

PARING KNIFE

Chef's Knife

HONING STEEL

OFFSET SERRATED KNIFE

How-to hone?
Go to: tccb.co
Or, using your
smartphone,
scan this image.

# GEAR UP.

Do you have a favorite pair of sweatpants that you put on when you get home from work that make you feel comfortable, cozy, and relaxed? Let's replicate that same feeling with your cooking gear.

Choose cutting boards that appeal to you (fun colors! large surface area!), knives that don't completely scare you (easy-to-hold handles! not too heavy!), and pots, pans, and bowls that look and feel nice (clear glass? plastic? nice shapes?). When you have gear that you like, comfort and even motivation will set in. It's like an exercise program—if you love your sneakers, your music, and even your outfit, aren't you more inclined to get into it? For your kitchen, I suggest putting on music that you enjoy, to both fuel and relax you. A glass of wine is also helpful to set a nice tone—the tone being you are going to enjoy yourself while you tackle something new.

## KNIVES

There is no way around it—knives are scary. I'm stating the obvious here, but knives are a big part of cooking. Knives are yet another obstacle for many people who are already afraid because they lack skills and experience. I am breaking it down to three knives that will help you start your little journey out of Can't Cooksville. Most experienced chefs will tell you they reach for only their three favorites when they are cooking. You, my friend, definitely don't need more than that. And believe it or not, a sharp knife is a safe knife. When your knife is sharp, it glides through food without force, so don't be afraid to use that honing steel.

One favor, please hand-wash your knives. And never throw them into the sink. Leave them on the side to be cleaned, so they don't get chipped or dulled by being tossed around.

### Paring Knife

Small and versatile, use this short-bladed knife for more precise tasks like peeling, trimming, and coring fruits and vegetables.

### Chef's Knife

The most useful and indispensable knife in the drawer, use it for slicing, smashing, and chopping. Choose between an 8-inch blade (the most common) and a 6-inch blade (for smaller hands). Comfort is key.

### Honing Steel

Keep your edge with a honing steel for weekly maintenance in between professional sharpenings (which I recommend doing about once a year).

### Offset Serrated Knife

The scalloped blade lets you glide through crusty breads and delicate tomatoes alike, slicing them instead of sliding off or crushing them. The offset handle keeps your knuckles out of harm's way.

RIMMED SHEET PAN ⇨

Large Baking Dish

Small, Medium, Large
**Skillets**

*Nonstick Skillet*

Large Pot with Lid 5- to 6-qt.

SAUCEPANS
SMALL & MEDIUM

⇦ LARGE POT
8- to 10-qt.

## POTS, PANS & SKILLETS

Buying pots and pans is an investment for sure, so let's take a streamlined approach to getting you what is most necessary. High-quality stainless steel cookware with aluminum or copper cores should last you a lifetime. You can buy a set—they are often on sale (nice!)—or you can consider what's offered below and buy as needed.

### Small Saucepan (2-qt.) with Lid

Great for melting butter, reheating soups, and making oatmeal or small batches of rice or grains.

### Medium Saucepan (3- to 4-qt.) with Lid

The perfectly sized utility pan for making sauces, cooking grains, or boiling potatoes.

### Large Pot (5- to 6-qt.) with Lid

Super for making soups, pasta sauce, and stews. Enameled cast iron and stainless steel are equally great.

### Large Pot (8- to 10-qt.) with Lid

Ideal for making large batches of soups, stocks, and sauces, but used mainly for cooking pasta.

### Small Skillet (8-inch)

Just the right size for toasting nuts or frying an egg.

### Medium Skillet (10-inch)

Fantastic for cooking meats or vegetables for two or four. Ovenproof is preferable.

### Large Skillet (12-inch)

Perfect for making pancakes or French toast, cooking large batches of vegetables, cooking pork chops or steaks, or roasting a chicken. Ovenproof is preferable.

### Medium Nonstick Skillet (10-inch)

Invaluable when it comes to scrambling eggs. It's recommended that it be used only over low to medium heat for short cooking times and that it be immediately disposed of if any scratches appear or if there is any other damage. This skillet is not ovenproof.

### Large Baking Dish or Roasting Pan (2½- to 3-qt.)

Terrific for roasting meats and vegetables, baking macaroni and cheese, or baking fruit crisps. Porcelain, glass, and stainless steel are all suitable.

### Rimmed Sheet Pan

One of the most versatile yet inexpensive pans in the kitchen. Choose a 13 x 18-inch (known as a half sheet pan) heavy-duty uncoated aluminum pan for roasting vegetables and meats as well as for baking cookies. So useful you might as well buy two.

COLANDER

Mixing bowls
small, medium, large

*Cutting Boards*

MEASURING CUPS

MEASURING SPOONS

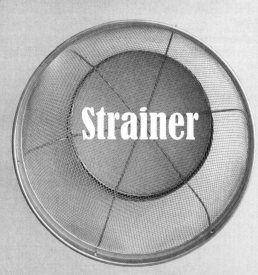

Strainer

Springform Pan

BAKING PAN

WIRE COOLING RACK ⇨

loaf pan

MUFFIN TIN

CAKE PAN

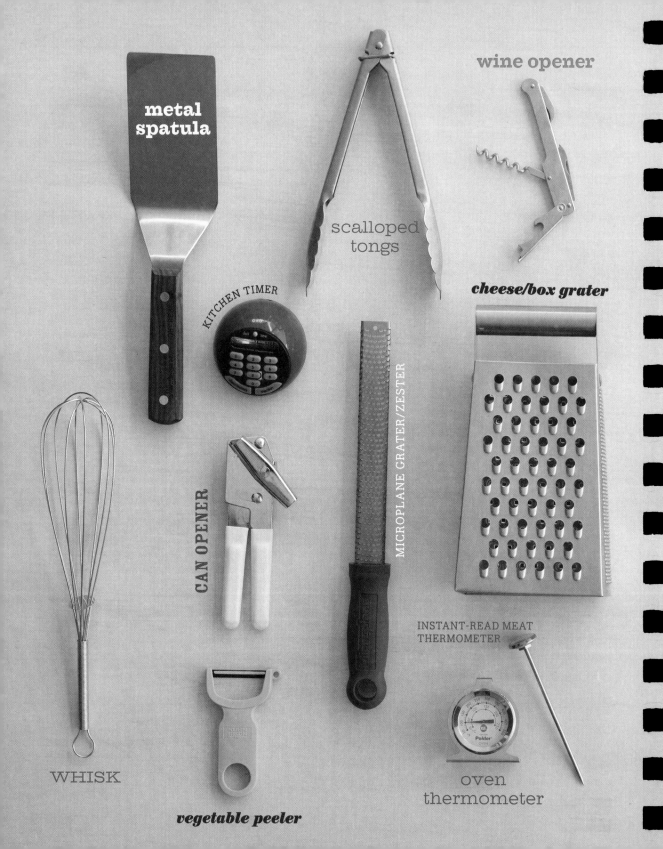

metal
spatula

scalloped
tongs

wine opener

KITCHEN TIMER

cheese/box grater

CAN OPENER

MICROPLANE GRATER/ZESTER

WHISK

vegetable peeler

INSTANT-READ MEAT
THERMOMETER

oven
thermometer

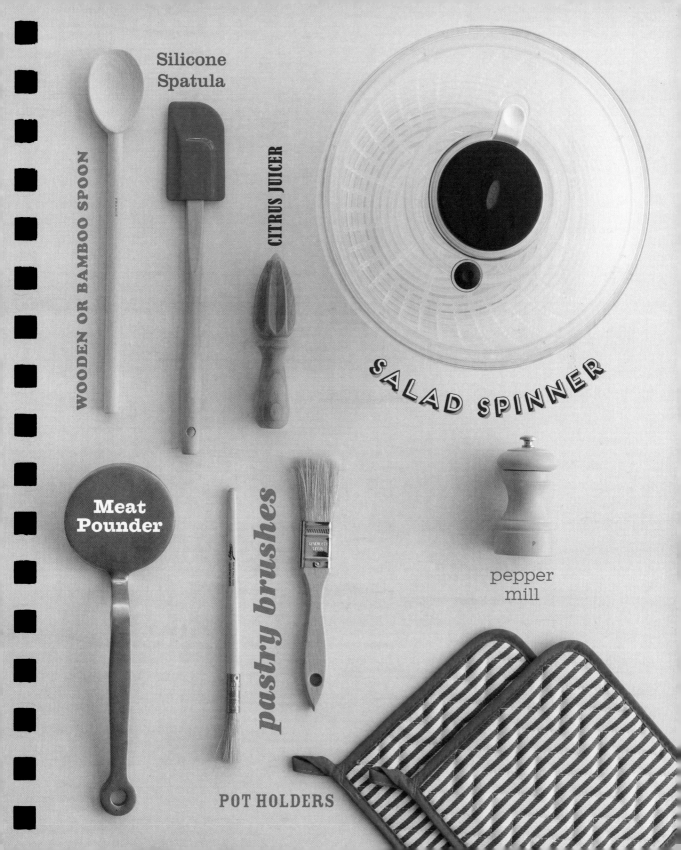

Silicone Spatula

WOODEN OR BAMBOO SPOON

CITRUS JUICER

SALAD SPINNER

pepper mill

**Meat Pounder**

*pastry brushes*

POT HOLDERS

## CUTTING BOARDS
### Large Cutting Board (15×21-inch)
Look for one with grippers to hold it in place. Wood, polypropylene, and the eco-friendly kind made from recycled paper are all terrific choices.

### Small Cutting Board (11×14-inch)
Ideal for smaller tasks and for those who don't have a lot of counter space.

## MIXING BOWLS, COLANDERS & STRAINERS
### Mixing Bowls
Some handy sizes: 1½-, 3½-, and 5-qt. Make sure you buy ones that nest for compact storage. Glass, melamine, and stainless are all great options.

### Colander
Perfect for draining pasta and washing/rinsing vegetables.

### Strainer
When a large colander is just too big for the task, use a fine-mesh strainer for rinsing a pint of cherry tomatoes or draining canned beans.

## MEASURING SPOONS
¼ tsp., ½ tsp., 1 tsp., and 1 T. sizes. Use for measuring both dry and liquid ingredients. Stainless steel, silicone, and melamine are all good choices.

## MEASURING CUPS
¼ c., ⅓ c., ½ c., and 1 c. sizes. Use for measuring dry ingredients like flour and sugar. Look for stainless steel, silicone, or melamine.

## LIQUID MEASURING CUPS
1 c., 2 c., and 4 c. sizes. Use these cups for measuring liquids. Buy glass, silicone, or plastic.

## GRATERS, PEELERS, OPENERS & TONGS
### Cheese/Box Grater
Buy a multipurpose grater that has coarse, fine, and superfine grating surfaces; perfect for grating anything from cheese to carrots to ginger.

### Microplane Grater/Zester
This razor-sharp grater is indispensable when it comes to grating citrus zest, hard cheeses, and whole nutmeg.

### Vegetable Peeler
I like a Y-shaped peeler.

### Can Opener
Buy one with sharp stainless steel teeth and large comfortable knob and handles to make it a little more effortless to open a can.

### Wine Opener
When it's wine o'clock, any simple wine opener will do.

### Scalloped Tongs
Tongs are one of the most useful tools in your kitchen. Use them for turning, lifting, stirring, grabbing . . . just about anything. I recommend ones that lock in a closed position. Both the 9-inch and the 12-inch are handy.

## THERMOMETERS & TIMERS
### Instant-Read Meat Thermometer
Takes the guesswork out of knowing when your meat is cooked to the temperature you want. It's inexpensive, too.

## Oven Thermometer
The secret to success, especially when baking, is knowing that your oven is the right temperature.

## Kitchen Timer
So you don't forgot those nuts that are toasting or the cookies that are baking!

## MORE TOOLS
### Salad Spinner
A must for washing and drying lettuce.

### Citrus Juicer
A wooden reamer is a low-cost, low-tech way to juice citrus.

### Meat Pounder
For pounding chicken breasts to an even thickness (a rolling pin works great for this, too).

### Pastry Brush
Not a necessity but convenient when you need to evenly coat something with oil (like the tortillas for Huevos Rancheros, page 55).

### Pepper Mill
There is nothing better than freshly ground black peppercorns. Choose a pepper mill that will adjust to any size grind you like.

### Pot Holders
Choose ones that can handle the heat and that are pliable for grabbing handles with ease. A folded-over dry dish towel will do the trick, too.

## SPATULAS & SPOONS
### Metal Spatula
Buy one with an offset handle and a flexible square-edged head to make lifting, serving, and flipping anything from burgers to pancakes a breeze.

## Silicone Spatula
Why silicone? Because it is flexible, heat-resistant, and durable, and it won't scratch your pan. Use for mixing, folding, spreading, and scraping a bowl clean.

## Wooden or Bamboo Spoon
Excellent for stirring and won't scratch the surface of enamel, porcelain, or nonstick cookware.

## Whisk
10-inch stainless steel is my choice.

## BAKING
### 12-cup Muffin Tin
For the standard size muffin or cupcake. Nonstick is perfectly fine.

### 9-inch Springform Pan
The pan's round ring springs free when the clamp is opened, making it easier to remove your baked goods.

### 9-inch Round Cake Pan
To turn out the perfect cake every time, buy a straight-sided aluminum pan. I avoid nonstick here as it can make your cake brown too quickly.

### 8 × 8-inch Baking Pan
Great for making brownies, cakes, and bar cookies. You can even use it for baking macaroni and cheese. Aluminum will last a lifetime.

### 8½ × 4½-inch Loaf Pan
Use this pan for baking meat loaves and banana breads alike. Opt for metal rather than glass.

### Wire Cooling Rack
Transfer you warm cakes or cookies to this rack so they cool quickly and evenly.

# The Terrifying
# FOOD PROCESSOR

Yes, it's loud, formidable, and a big piece of equipment, but it's also very handy when it comes to chopping. Let's do it together, so you have a good experience.

First, put the base on a stable surface, then lock the bowl in place. Then, slide in the metal blade and add your ingredient(s). For something large like a tomato or an onion, cut it into quarters first. Lock in the top. Press the Pulse button several times in quick succession to chop. The Pulse button gives you more control than the On button, which can quickly turn that onion you're trying to chop into mush. You can use the On button for pureeing vegetables or for making pesto.

# RECOMMENDED APPLIANCES

You will come across a few recipes where electrical appliances are needed. Take your time to buy them. The recipes aren't going anywhere. Buy what you can. Think of this as a long-term investment.

11-c. Food Processor

Blender

5- to 6-qt. Slow Cooker

Panini Press

Toaster

Electric Mixer

# STOCK UP.

On any given day, there are lots of things conspiring to prevent you from cooking a good meal. I'm going to show you how to remove one of the easiest reasons: not having the basic cooking essentials on hand.

You can't get dressed without some clothes in your closet, and it works the same way in the kitchen. Setting up a foundation of ingredients you can use (and use again) is a game changer. For me, that includes these key items: olive oil, kosher salt, freshly ground pepper, Parmesan, fresh garlic, fresh herbs, and fresh lemon. Think of these as your "wardrobe essentials."

I have tried hard to keep the recipes very simple by using few ingredients. I took this approach because I find for busy, intimidated Can't Cooks, fewer ingredients mean fewer steps. As you will see in this book, I hold olive oil in high regard. I tend to cook with a basic, not-too-expensive extra virgin olive oil that's mild in flavor. Sometimes I splurge on a special extra virgin olive oil with a more pronounced olive flavor for dipping bread and making vinaigrettes. When you see e.v. olive oil in the recipes, know that it means extra virgin olive oil.

As far as kosher salt goes, I prefer it over regular table salt because the crystals are bigger, making it easier to pinch. To me the flavor of kosher salts blends better with foods and tastes more balanced.

I also want to make a case for grinding fresh black pepper versus buying it already ground. Using a pepper mill with fresh peppercorns or cracking peppercorns by hand (see How-to, page 38) makes a big difference in flavor. On that note, I encourage you to look at your spice rack (if you have one) and consider updating your supply. If your spices have been in your life since the '90s, it's time to replace them with new ones.

Chopping your own garlic and using fresh lemons for zest and juice will also produce a higher-quality result for you. Please resist the urge to buy garlic pre-chopped or lemons pre-juiced—the flavor just doesn't compare. You'll be ahead of the game if you start off using wholesome, unprocessed ingredients.

Organic is great to buy, but it's not in everyone's budget. It's your choice on where you spend, but if I could put my two cents in, I'd love to see you work with high-quality (i.e., better-tasting) organic ingredients when you can. When you cook with excellent ingredients, you are elevating your potential for making a flavorful, fresh-tasting meal.

# SET UP.

Can I offer you a shortcut to success? Believe it or not, the key to all of this madness is to be organized before you start. You WILL BE successful if you have the same basic setup every time you cook. Rushing around and looking for things just creates chaos and stress. I call this initial part "Getting Your Sh#t Together."

**1** Set up a cutting board. (If your board doesn't have grippers on the bottom, place a wet paper towel underneath to prevent the board from slipping.)

**2** Take out your knife and place it on the board.

**3** Place your measuring spoons and cups nearby.

**4** Set out the salt, pepper mill, and olive oil.

**5** Have your canister of utensils nearby.

**6** Keep a dry dish towel and paper towels handy.

**7** Set out a small plate to use for dirty spoons.

Now go to your recipe and read it through COMPLETELY before you start. Set out the specific pots and pans and ingredients listed so you can easily reach for what you need. Believe it or not, you're ready to start cooking.

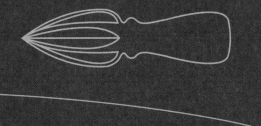

# How-to.

Everything that might put you in Panic Mode is dealt with head-on, right here in this section. When you are ready to attempt a recipe, and a step or two frightens you, come back to these pages. More than likely there will be a solution for you. There is no challenge we can't get through together. **I am trying to give you as much instruction as possible without freaking you out with too much detail.**

**The photos and instructions that follow practically do the work for you. If you want even more support, visit www.tccb.co for my How-to videos. Or if you want to get all tech-y, you can access the videos using an exciting feature called digital watermarking. Simply download the free app at scannow.mobi/tccb then hold your phone's camera a few inches away from the photo with the video icon next to it and help is on the way.**

How-to? Go to: tccb.co

# Citrus: How-to

I can't get enough citrus. It's a no-fat, high-flavor way to zip up any dish.
You can zest it or juice it and add it to most things for a light, bright flavor.

*wash*

*grate the zest*

## prep it

**Wash** and dry the outside of the lemon, lime, or orange.

*Depending on the recipe, you may need citrus zest, juice, or both. If you need both, zest the citrus first.*

## zest it

The colorful outer layer of the peel of citrus is called the zest. To zest it means to capture this flavorful layer by grating it. **Grate the zest** by moving the citrus in one direction along a grater/ zester, pressing and rotating as you go and removing only the colorful outer layer. Stop when you get to the white part. Turn the citrus and repeat until you have the amount you want.

Zest of 1 lemon = about 1 tsp.
Zest of 1 lime = about ½ tsp.
Zest of 1 orange = about 1 T.

How-to? Go to: **tccb.co**
Or, using your smartphone, scan the images with the video icon.

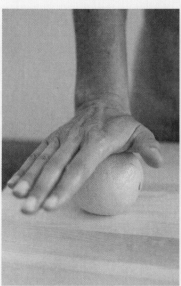

*firmly press and roll*        *cut in half crosswise*         *push and twist*

# juice it

To juice it, first **firmly press and roll** the citrus back and forth on your work surface to get its juices flowing. **Cut in half crosswise** and flick out any visible seeds. Insert the citrus reamer (or the tines of a fork) into the center of the fruit and **push and twist** to extract the juice (you may have to scoop out any stray seeds).

Juice from 1 lemon = about 3 T.
Juice from 1 lime = 1 to 2 T.
Juice from 1 orange = ⅓ to ½ c.

# Garlic: How-to

If you learn one thing, learn how to use fresh garlic. Nothing beats it.
Depending on the recipe, you'll use it smashed or chopped.

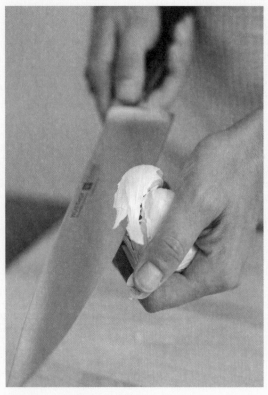

*twist your knife to pop it out*

*use one quick pounding motion*

## remove a clove

To remove a clove of garlic from a garlic bulb,
slide your knife between the cloves, then **twist
your knife to pop it out**.

## smash it

Place the garlic clove on your cutting board.
Place the side of your chef's knife on top of it and
smash it with your open palm. (**Use one quick
pounding motion**.) The harder you smash your
garlic cloves, the easier they will be to peel and
chop.

How-to? Go to: **tccb.co**
Or, using your smartphone, scan
the images with the video icon.

*peel away the papery outer layer*

*use a seesaw action*

# peel it

The smashing action works to loosen the garlic
clove's skin. Use your fingers to **peel away the
papery outer layer**. Cut off and discard brown
ends. It's okay if the smashed garlic pieces are
different sizes.

# chop it

To chop the cloves, hold the handle of the chef's
knife with one hand and place your other hand
(fingers extended) on top of the opposite end
of the knife. With the knife running through the
garlic, **use a seesaw action** to rock the blade
back and forth until the garlic is chopped into
small pieces.

# Onion: How-to

For all you Can't Cooks out there, let's face the onion together. It's far less intimidating than you might think and essential to so many recipes.

*trim off the stem end*     *cut the onion in half*     *peel away*

## prep it

Place the onion on your cutting board. **Trim off the stem end** of the onion—not the hairy root end. Rest the onion on the flat end you've just created and **cut the onion in half** from root end to stem end. **Peel away** the papery outer layer. You're now ready to slice or chop your onion.

How-to? Go to: **tccb.co**
Or, using your smartphone, scan the images with the video icon.

*Depending on the recipe, you will either slice OR chop your onions.*

*slice into half-moons*

*slice into it lengthwise*

*make even, perpendicular cuts*

# slice it

Prep your onion (**trim**, **cut in half**, and **peel**). Then lay one half of the onion flat on your cutting board. Starting at the trimmed end, and with the backs of your fingers up against the blade and your fingertips tucked back and away, thinly **slice into half-moons**, stopping short of the root. Repeat with the other half.

# chop it

Prep your onion (**trim**, **cut in half**, and **peel**). Then lay one half of the onion flat on your cutting board. Starting on one side, **slice into it lengthwise** toward the center of the onion (think, rays of the sun) at ¼- to ½-inch intervals to just near, but not through, the root end (you need the root end intact to hold everything together). Slice all the way around the onion. Then change your blade direction and **make even, perpendicular cuts** until you reach the root end. The chopped pieces will fall away as you cut. Chop it into smaller pieces after that, if you like. Repeat with the other half.

# Shallots: How-to

A shallot is a small onion, only a little milder and sweeter. Great when chopped in vinaigrettes or thinly sliced as in Bread Crumb Bass (p. 113).

*thinly slice*

*slice into it lengthwise*

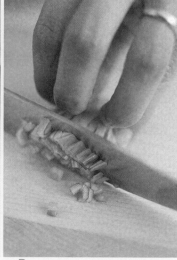

*make perpendicular cuts*

## slice it

First prep your shallot by cutting off the stem end and peeling away the papery outer layer. With the backs of your fingers up against the blade and your fingertips tucked back and away, **thinly slice** the shallot into rings until you reach the root end.

## chop it

First prep your shallot by cutting off the stem end and peeling away the papery outer layer. **Slice into it lengthwise** at even intervals to just near, but not through, the root end. Change your blade direction and **make perpendicular cuts** across the shallot until you reach the stem end. (Be sure that you chop safely by keeping the backs of your fingers up against the blade and your fingertips tucked back and away.) The pieces will fall away as you cut.

# Scallions: How-to

Also known as green onions. An easy way to flavor up a dish without too much hassle.

*cut off the hairy root end*

*peel the outer membrane*

*thinly slice*

## prep it

Place the scallion on your cutting board. **Cut off the hairy root end** and discard. **Peel the outer membrane** of the scallion and discard that as well. Wash. Now you're ready to slice.

How-to? Go to: tccb.co
Or, using your smartphone, scan the images with the video icon.

## slice it

With the backs of your fingers up against the blade and your fingertips tucked back and away, **thinly slice** the white and light green parts while the tip of the knife remains on the cutting board. If you're up to it, you can slice a few scallions at a time. Stop slicing when you get to the dark green part, which you can discard, as it can be bitter.

# Herbs: How-to

Fresh herbs can enhance just about any dish. I use them all the time. Here are the basics so that you can, too.

*pick the leaves*

*pinch your fingers around the top of the sprig, gently strip/pull*

## pick it

Rinse leafy herbs such as sage, cilantro, and parsley under cool running water and **pat dry** with a paper towel. **Pick the leaves** from the stems and place in a pile on your cutting board. You're now ready to either use the leaves whole or chop them.

## strip it

Rinse robust herbs such as rosemary and thyme under cool running water and **pat dry** with a paper towel. **Pinch your fingers around the top of the sprig.** Then **gently strip/pull** the leaves from the sprig in the opposite direction from how they grow. You're now ready to **chop the leaves or use them whole**.

*I usually tear mint and basil leaves instead of chopping them. This avoids bruising (and you don't have to use your knife!).*

*chop the leaves or use them whole* 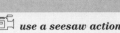 *use a seesaw action*     *wrap them (unwashed)*

## chop it

To chop, place the leaves in a pile on your cutting board. Hold the handle of your chef's knife with one hand and place your other hand (fingers extended) on top of the opposite end of the knife. With the knife blade running through the pile of leaves, **use a seesaw action** to rock the knife back and forth until the herbs are chopped into small pieces.

How-to? Go to: **tccb.co**
Or, using your smartphone, scan the images with the video icon.

## store it

If not using herbs right away, **wrap them (unwashed)** in a dry paper towel and place in a plastic bag (leave it unsealed). Store in the crisper drawer of your refrigerator.

# Avocado: How-to

A gem of a snack. Learn how to safely remove the pit, scoop it, slice it, dice it, or just eat it right out of its skin.

*cut into, twist*

*give it a firm whack*

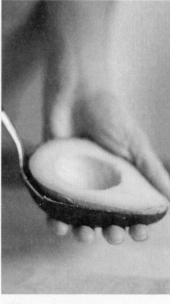

*slide in a large spoon*

## prep it

Put the avocado on your cutting board and place your palm flat over the top. With your chef's knife horizontal to the board, **cut into** the avocado until you reach the pit. Hold the knife still while you rotate the avocado to cut all the way around the pit. Remove the knife. **Twist** the two halves apart.

To remove the pit, aim the bottom edge of the blade at the pit and **give it a firm whack** to lodge the knife into the pit (if this freaks you out, scoop out the pit with a spoon). Twist the knife and pull out the pit. Flick off the pit with your thumb. You're now ready to scoop out whole, slice, or dice the avocado.

## scoop it

**Slide in a large spoon** between the flesh and the skin of the avocado, and scoop it out. Try to get all the flesh out in one shot.

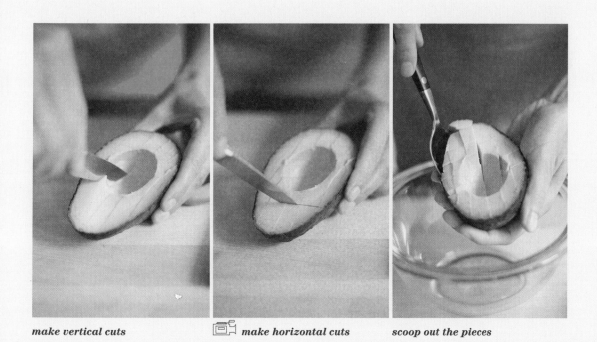

*make vertical cuts*　　　 *make horizontal cuts*　　　*scoop out the pieces*

# slice & dice it

Prep the avocado by cutting it in half and removing the pit. Place the two halves, cut side up, on the cutting board. Without cutting through the avocado skin, use the tip of your paring knife to carefully **make vertical cuts** into the avocado flesh. If you just want slices, scoop them out now.

If you want diced avocado, **make horizontal cuts** in addition to the vertical cuts. Then you're ready to **scoop out the pieces**.

How-to? Go to: **tccb.co**
Or, using your smartphone, scan the images with the video icon.

# Carrots: How-to

Cutting up carrots is great practice for your knife skills. In some recipes you'll need carrots cut into sticks, and in others, chopped into pieces.

*cut across, then cut lengthwise*

*lay it flat side down, cut in half lengthwise*

*cut crosswise*

## make sticks

First, peel the carrot. Then place it on your cutting board and trim away the root end. **Cut across** the carrot so it's half its original length. (If your carrot is particularly long, cut across into thirds.) Now, holding one end of the carrot half, carefully **cut lengthwise** in half. **Lay it flat side down** on the cutting board. Then **cut in half lengthwise** again. Repeat. Now you have carrot sticks.

## chop

To chop, stack your carrot sticks together. Then, with the backs of your fingers up against the blade and your fingertips tucked back and away, **cut crosswise** while the tip of the knife remains on the cutting board. The pieces will fall away as you go.

How-to? Go to: **tccb.co**
Or, using your smartphone, scan the images with the video icon.

# Nuts: How-to

For the Broiled Honey-Nut Bananas (p. 213), you'll need chopped walnuts. And in more than one recipe you'll toast either almonds or pine nuts.

*keep the knife tip down*

*stir or shake the nuts often*

## chop

First, gather the nuts in a pile on your cutting board. Then hold the handle of the chef's knife with one hand and place your other hand (fingers extended) on top of the opposite end of the knife. **Keep the knife tip down** on the cutting board (this will create stability) while rocking the blade back and forth through the nuts. As you chop, keep gathering the nuts into a pile by sliding them together with the knife.

## toast

To toast sliced almonds or pine nuts, place a small dry skillet on the stove and add the nuts. Turn the heat to medium. **Stir or shake the nuts often** in the skillet (so they cook evenly) until lightly toasted and fragrant, 3 to 5 minutes. Remove from the heat.

# Salt & Pepper: How-to

Learn here how to enhance the flavor of your meals with salt and pepper.

## freshly cracked pepper

Why am I asking you to do this? If you like pepper, you'll love it freshly cracked even more. You just can't beat the boldness of the flavor it delivers. I'm not saying you need to do this for every recipe, but it's stellar for steak (p. 89) and cacio e pepe (p. 137). I keep whole peppercorns on hand all the time and crack them as needed.

To get started, pour some peppercorns onto your cutting board. Using the bottom of a small skillet's round edge, **firmly press down to crack the peppercorns**. (Make sure they are all cracked before adding to the recipe—you might break a tooth!)

How-to? Go to: **tccb.co**
Or, using your smartphone, scan
the images with the video icon.

*sprinkle evenly*

*add a pinch, to suit your palate*

# season with salt

This is an important first step for you. Measure
the salt (or other seasoning) with a measuring
spoon and pour into the palm of your hand. With
your other hand, pinch and then **sprinkle evenly**
over your food before cooking.

# season to taste

Sometimes at the end of a recipe you will note
the term "season to taste." What does this
mean? Simply put, you may want to **add a pinch**
of salt and/or pepper (too small to measure with
measuring spoons) **to suit your palate**. Start by
adding a tiny pinch and/or a turn of your pepper
mill. Give it a try. Add more if your taste buds call
for it.

# Shrimp: How-to

You can always buy shrimp that have already been peeled and deveined, but that can be expensive. Here's the know-how to do it yourself.

*peel away the shell*

*gently cut into the back*

*rinse*

## peel it

This action is best done in the sink, with a colander standing by in which to place your peeled shrimp. **Peel away the shell**. (You can leave the tail on or remove it completely.) I recommend that you peel all of your shrimp first before moving on to the next step, deveining.

## devein it

Hold the shrimp securely in one hand with the curved back of the shrimp facing outward. With your other hand, use a paring knife to **gently cut into** (but not through) **the back** to expose the vein. **Rinse** under cold running water while you pull out the vein. You're ready to cook your shrimp!

*To check for ocean-friendly seafood, visit the Monterey Bay Aquarium's Seafood Watch website.*
**montereybayaquarium.org**

# Fish: How-to

How-to? Go to: tccb.co
Or, using your smartphone, scan
the images with the video icon.

No question about it—it can be intimidating
to know when fish is done. Here's how.
Don't be afraid.

## check it

To check fish for doneness, **insert the tip of a paring knife** into
the thickest part of the fish and gently twist. If it flakes easily and looks
opaque in the center, then it is done.

*Some fish is sold with its skin on. Salmon, in particular,
is delicious cooked that way. If it upsets you to have skin,
ask the person who sells you fish to skin it (and remove pin
bones) for you.*

# Flour: How-to

Who knew there was a right and wrong way to measure flour? The key here is not to pack your flour when you measure it. Keep it light and fluffy.

*fluff it*     *spoon it*    *level it*

## measure it

Before you do anything with the flour, **fluff it** with a large spoon. Then, to measure, the best method is to **spoon it** into your measuring cup (do not pack), then **level it** off with a knife. This will keep the flour nice and fluffy rather than packed and heavy, which can throw off a recipe.

How-to? Go to: **tccb.co**
Or, using your smartphone, scan the images with the video icon.

# Wash: How-to

Just like washing your hands, washing fruits, vegetables, chicken, and fish is a good habit to get into to rinse away pesticides and germs.

*rinse it*

*gently scrub*

*agitate the water*

## chicken & fish

To clean chicken or fish, **rinse it** under cool running water. Pat completely dry with paper towels. I generally don't wash pork, beef, or lamb, but simply pat it dry; it will form a better crust this way.

## produce

Pass vegetables and fruit under cool running water and **gently scrub** with your fingers to remove dirt and wash away germs. Shake or **pat dry**.

## greens

To wash greens like lettuce, spinach, and kale, start by tearing large leaves into bite-size pieces, then put them into a salad spinner. Fill the spinner with cold water and **agitate the water** with your hands to free dirt from the greens. Lift out the strainer. Dump out the water—you may have to rinse again if the greens are especially dirty. Put the top on the spinner and spin out the greens so that they are dry.

# Breakfast

SCRAMBLED EGGS & CREAM CHEESE

FRIED EGGS OVER BROILED TOMATOES

**Soft-boiled Eggs with Toast**

Sweet Pea & Onion Frittata

Huevos Rancheros

Shepherd's French Toast

LEMON RICOTTA PANCAKES

BANANA-DATE BRAN MUFFINS

Fresh Berry Crumb Cake

# SCRAMBLED EGGS & CREAM CHEESE

This is my mom's recipe. It gives that half-used block of cream cheese in your fridge an exciting second life.

8 large eggs
2 T. cream cheese
2 T. water
⅛ tsp. kosher salt
⅛ tsp. freshly ground black pepper
½ T. unsalted butter
Fresh dill sprigs (optional), in honor of my grandmother, who is a dill lover

**Tools needed:** medium bowl, paring knife, measuring spoons, whisk or fork, medium nonstick skillet, silicone spatula.

**Don't Panic:** Not overcooking the eggs is definitely something you can handle.

1. **Crack** the eggs into a medium bowl. **Measure** the cream cheese, **cut** up into small pieces, and **add** to the eggs. Then **add** the water, salt, and pepper (about 6 turns on a pepper mill) **Ⓐ**. Using a whisk or fork, **beat** until the eggs are an even yellow with the bits of cream cheese still visible.

2. **Place** your medium nonstick skillet on the stove and **turn** the heat to medium. **Add** the butter. Once it's melted, **swirl** the skillet so the butter coats the bottom. **Pour in** the eggs and **let sit** untouched for 30 seconds.

3. Then, using a silicone spatula, slowly **scrape** the bottom of the pan, working from the edges to the center. The eggs will start to come together. Continuously, but gently, **scrape** and **turn** the eggs over themselves until they are done to your liking (you do not want them to brown) **Ⓑ**. **Serve** 'em up. **Tear** the dill and **sprinkle** over the eggs, if you like.

Ⓐ

Ⓑ

# FRIED EGGS OVER BROILED TOMATOES

I have no problem serving this as a quick breakfast, lunch, or dinner at my house alongside a slice of crusty country bread drizzled with olive oil.

1 large beefsteak tomato
1 T. plus 2 tsp. e.v. olive oil
¼ tsp. dried oregano
¼ tsp. kosher salt (⅛ tsp. + ⅛ tsp.)
Freshly ground black pepper
2 large eggs
2 T. grated Parmesan

Tools needed: cutting board, chef's knife, rimmed sheet pan, measuring spoons, medium skillet, metal spatula, cheese grater (if grating it yourself).

Don't Panic: Using the broiler for the tomato slices and frying the eggs on the stovetop to your preferred doneness may cause you concern. Don't fret—we'll work this out.

1. **Heat** the broiler (with the oven rack about 4 inches from the top). **Slice** the tomato into four ½-inch-thick rounds Ⓐ and **place** on a rimmed sheet pan. **Measure** 1 T. of the oil and **drizzle** over the slices. **Measure** the oregano, then **pinch** and **sprinkle** over the slices; **do** the same with ⅛ tsp. of the salt. **Season** each slice with a turn on the pepper mill. **Broil** until the tomato has softened slightly, 2 to 3 minutes. **Divide** between two plates.

Ⓐ

2. **Place** your medium skillet on the stove and **turn** the heat to medium-low. **Measure** and **pour** in the remaining 2 tsp. oil and **heat** until it shimmers (1 to 2 minutes). **Swirl** the skillet so the oil coats the bottom.

3. **Crack** each egg and **open** about 2 inches above the skillet so the egg slides gently out; space them a few inches apart. **Cook** until the whites are set (not runny) and the yolks are still soft to the touch, 2 to 3 minutes. For an "over easy" egg, carefully **flip** with a spatula and **cook** for 30 seconds more. Gently **lift** each egg out of the skillet while being careful not to break the yolk. **Serve** on top of the tomato slices. **Season** the eggs with the remaining ⅛ tsp. salt and pepper to taste and **sprinkle** with the Parmesan.

# Soft-boiled Eggs with Toast a.k.a. The Granny Egg

My grandmother made these for me my whole life. So simple, so good.

French, country, or whole
    wheat bread
4 large eggs
1 T. unsalted butter
Kosher salt and freshly
    ground black pepper,
    to taste

Tools needed: medium
saucepan, cutting board,
serrated knife, large spoon,
toaster, kitchen timer.

\*How-to:
    Season to taste, p. 39

Don't Panic: You can learn to boil an egg. I know you can.

1. **Fill** a medium saucepan with water (about 2 inches from the top) and **place** on the stove. **Turn** the heat to medium-high and let the water come to a boil. While it comes to a boil, **slice** the bread into two ½-inch-thick slices if not using presliced.

2. Once the water is boiling, **use** a large spoon to carefully **lower** the eggs, one at a time, into the water. **Lower** the heat and gently **simmer** (low boil) for 5½ minutes. **Set** your timer.

3. While the eggs simmer, **toast** the bread in your toaster until golden brown, then **spread** the tops with butter. **Cut** each piece of toast into small squares and **put** into individual bowls.

4. After 5½ minutes, **pour** out the hot water from the pan. Immediately **crack** each egg by tapping and rotating it several times on the edge of the sink. Because they are hot to handle, **pass** them under cold running water while you gently peel  **Ⓐ**.

5. **Place** the eggs on top of the toast squares and **cut** them up so the yolks spill out. **Gently toss. Season** with salt and pepper to taste.\*

Ⓐ

# Sweet Pea & Onion Frittata

You can get creative here without fear. Use any vegetable you have in your fridge: just add to the cooked onions and then cook until tender; chopped spinach and zucchini work well. While you're at it, throw in a chopped fresh herb.

1 large yellow onion
2 T. e.v. olive oil
1 tsp. kosher salt (½ tsp. +
    ½ tsp.)
8 large eggs
¼ c. grated Parmesan, plus
    more for sprinkling
¼ tsp. freshly ground black
    pepper
1 c. frozen peas

Tools needed: cutting board, chef's knife, medium ovenproof skillet, measuring cups and spoons, tongs, whisk or fork, medium bowl, cheese grater (if grating it yourself), strainer, kitchen timer.

*How-to:
    Slice an onion, p. 29

Don't Panic: Yes, you are using both the stovetop *and* the oven. You are also going to multitask, but it's manageable.

1. **Heat** the oven (with the oven rack in the middle) to 350°F.

2. Thinly **slice** the onion into half-moons.*

3. **Place** your medium ovenproof skillet on the stove and **turn** the heat to medium. **Measure** and **pour** in the oil and **heat** until it shimmers (1 to 2 minutes). **Add** the onion and ½ tsp. of the salt and **cook**, turning often with tongs, until light golden brown and tender, 8 to 10 minutes Ⓐ. **Remove** from the heat and **spread** the onion evenly over the bottom of the skillet.

Ⓐ

4. While the onion cooks, **crack** the eggs into a medium bowl. Using a whisk or a fork, **beat** together until they are an even yellow. **Mix** in the Parmesan, pepper (about 12 turns on a pepper mill), and the remaining ½ tsp. salt.

5. To thaw the peas, **place** them in a strainer and **pass** under warm water, about 1 minute.

6. **Pour** the egg mixture over the onion and **scatter** the peas over the eggs. **Sprinkle** a small handful of extra Parmesan over the top and **transfer** the skillet to the oven. **Bake** until the middle is just set, 15 to 20 minutes.

# Huevos Rancheros

Do me a favor? Make this. Please use a hearty, rich, high-quality salsa. Thank you.

4 corn tortillas

1 T. e.v. olive oil

1 small head romaine lettuce

1 can (15.5-oz.) black or pinto refried beans

2 c. of your favorite salsa

4 large eggs

**Tools needed:** rimmed sheet pan, small bowl, pastry brush, cutting board, chef's knife, salad spinner, can opener, spoon, measuring cups and spoons, small saucepan, medium skillet with lid, kitchen timer.

**Don't Panic:** There are a few things going on at once, but it's all timed out for you. Cooking the egg in salsa may be a new thing, but you'll find there's really nothing to it.

1. **Heat** the oven (with the oven rack in the middle) to 400°F. **Place** the tortillas on a rimmed sheet pan. **Pour** the oil into a small bowl, then **brush** each side of the tortillas with the oil (if you don't have a brush, wing it with a paper towel). **Bake** until golden brown and crisp, 10 to 12 minutes.

2. While the tortillas bake, **tear** off and **discard** any discolored outer leaves from the head of lettuce. Then, starting at the leafy end, thinly **slice** it crosswise until you get about 2 c. of shredded lettuce. Or just **tear** it. **Place** in a salad spinner, **wash**, and **spin** dry.

3. **Place** a small saucepan on the stove and **add** the beans. **Turn** the heat to low and cook, stirring occasionally, until heated through.

4. While the beans heat, **place** a medium skillet on the stove and **add** the salsa. **Turn** the heat to medium. Once the salsa starts to bubble, **use** a spoon to make four small wells in the salsa, evenly spaced apart. **Crack** an egg into each well . **Cover** and **cook** until the whites are just set and the yolks are still soft to the touch, 3 to 5 minutes.

🅐

5. To assemble, **place** a tortilla on a plate and **layer** with some of the beans and lettuce. **Top** with one of the eggs and some of the salsa.

# Shepherd's French Toast

I am convinced that because my seven-year-old can make this, you can too.

2 large eggs
1 c. low-fat or whole milk
2 tsp. pure vanilla extract
¼ tsp. ground cinnamon
4 (1-inch-thick) slices
   challah or French bread
   (or whole wheat bread)
1 T. unsalted butter
Fresh berries, maple syrup,
   or confectioners' sugar,
   for serving

Tools needed: large
baking dish, measuring
cups and spoons, whisk
or fork, cutting board,
serrated knife, large skillet,
metal spatula.

Don't Panic: Flipping the French toast when ready is your calling.

1. **Crack** the eggs into a large baking dish (large enough to hold the bread slices in a single layer). **Add** the milk, vanilla, and cinnamon and **whisk** together. **Slice** the bread into 1-inch-thick slices (if not presliced) and **add** to the egg mixture. Let them **soak** for a minute, then **flip** each piece and let **soak** a minute more until saturated Ⓐ.

Ⓐ

Ⓑ

2. **Place** a large skillet on the stove and **turn** the heat to medium. **Add** the butter. Once it's melted, **swirl** the skillet so the butter coats the bottom. Let the excess egg mixture **drip** off of each slice of bread, then **add** the bread to the skillet (you may have to cook in batches if your bread is too wide to fit all 4 slices in at once) Ⓑ. **Listen** for a nice sizzle. When you hear that, **cook** until the undersides are golden brown, 2 to 3 minutes. Carefully **flip** and **cook** until golden on the second side, 2 to 3 minutes more. **Serve** with your favorite toppings.

# LEMON RICOTTA PANCAKES

Pancakes are my most favorite food. I say it's worth the extra steps to make them fresh, from scratch, as opposed to using a mix. This lemon ricotta version makes it worth getting out of bed.

½ c. all-purpose flour
½ c. whole wheat flour
2 T. sugar
2 tsp. baking powder
½ tsp. kosher salt
2 large eggs
1 c. low-fat or whole milk
½ c. whole milk or
    part-skim ricotta cheese
½ tsp. pure vanilla extract
Grated zest of ½ lemon
    (about ½ tsp.)
2 T. unsalted butter (½ T. +
    ½ T. + ½ T. + ½ T.)
Maple syrup, for serving

**Tools needed:** medium bowl, measuring cups and spoons, grater/zester, whisk, large skillet, metal spatula.

**\*How-to:**
    Measure flour, p. 42
    Zest citrus, p. 24

**Don't Panic:** Measuring and pouring the batter and flipping the pancakes at the right moment is simple stuff.

1. In a medium bowl, **measure** and **whisk** together the flours,**\*** sugar, baking powder, and salt (dry ingredients). **Add** the eggs, milk, ricotta, and vanilla (wet ingredients). **Grate** the **zest** directly into the bowl.**\*** **Whisk** everything together (do not overmix).

2. **Place** your large skillet on the stove and **turn** the heat to medium. **Add** ½ T. of the butter. Once it's melted, **swirl** the skillet so the butter coats the bottom of the pan. **Spoon in** 2 T. of batter for each pancake—**space** them a few inches apart because they will spread (a large skillet will hold 4 pancakes per batch).

3. **Cook** until bubbles on the tops of the pancakes start to pop and the undersides are golden, 1 to 2 minutes . **Flip** with a metal spatula, **cook** 30 seconds more, then **transfer** to a plate. **Repeat** with the remaining butter and batter (you may have to turn the heat down if the skillet becomes too hot and the pancakes start to scorch). **Serve** with maple syrup.

Ⓐ

# BANANA-DATE BRAN MUFFINS

You are going to make these with wheat bran, which is easy for beginners to work with and can be found in the flour section of a specialty grocery store. Keep some ripe bananas in the freezer so you can whip these up anytime (just thaw first). P.S.—No added sugar in these babies.

Cooking spray
½ c. walnut halves
3 ripe bananas
1 c. (packed full) pitted dates (Deglet or Medjool)
1 c. light buttermilk
¼ c. canola oil
1 c. wheat bran
1 c. all-purpose flour
1 tsp. ground cinnamon
¼ tsp. ground or grated whole nutmeg (about 12 passes on a grater)
1½ tsp. baking powder
½ tsp. baking soda
½ tsp. kosher salt

Tools needed: 12-cup muffin tin, food processor, measuring cups and spoons, large bowl, grater/ zester, whisk, silicone spatula, kitchen timer, wire rack.

*How-to:
   Use a food processor, p. 16
   Measure flour, p. 42

Don't Panic: Using the food processor (to puree the dates and bananas) is a big step forward. I think you're ready.

1. **Heat** the oven (with the oven rack in the middle) to 350°F. **Coat** the inside of the 12 cups of a muffin tin with cooking spray.

2. **Place** the nuts in a food processor and **pulse** a few times to roughly **chop** into small but not fine pieces.* **Transfer** to a small bowl. There is no need to wash the food processor yet.

3. **Peel** the bananas, **break** in half, and **place** them and the dates in the food processor. **Turn on** and let it run until smooth (puree). **Add** the buttermilk and oil and **pulse** a few times to combine.

4. In a large bowl, **measure** and **whisk** together the wheat bran, flour,* cinnamon, nutmeg, baking powder, baking soda, and salt (dry ingredients). Using a silicone spatula, **scrape** the banana mixture (wet ingredients) into the dry ingredients and **stir** until just combined. Do not overmix. **Stir** in ¼ c. of the chopped nuts, saving the rest to sprinkle on the tops.

5. **Spoon** the batter into the muffin cups, filling each cup two-thirds full. **Sprinkle** the tops with the remaining nuts. **Bake** until a toothpick inserted into the center comes out clean, 18 to 20 minutes. **Let cool** on a wire rack for 5 minutes before unmolding.

# CHICKEN

**Pan-Roasted Chicken Breasts**

SKILLET-ROASTED POTATOES & CHICKEN

Chicken with Rice & Peas

ROSEMARY CHICKEN UNDER A "BRICK"

FAST & JUICY HERB-GRILLED CHICKEN

Crispy Chicken Cutlets with Arugula & Lemon

ROASTED CHICKEN, SWEET POTATOES & TOMATOES

Sweet & Spicy Chicken Wings

ROASTED CHICKEN DRUMSTICKS—4 EASY RECIPES!

Seriously Basic Roast Chicken

# Pan-Roasted Chicken Breasts

I will not let you screw up these nice, juicy breasts. They are too easy not to make, even for a Can't Cook. If you don't have fresh thyme handy, any dried herb like thyme or oregano will do just fine (but use half the amount).

4 boneless, skinless chicken breasts (6 to 8 oz. each)

3 tsp. e.v. olive oil (1 tsp. + 2 tsp.)

½ tsp. kosher salt (¼ tsp. + ¼ tsp.)

¼ tsp. freshly ground black pepper (⅛ tsp. + ⅛ tsp.)

1 T. fresh thyme leaves (about 4 sprigs)

Tools needed: cutting board, chef's knife, measuring spoons, large skillet, tongs, kitchen timer.

Don't Panic: Knowing when the chicken is cooked through is NOT going to intimidate *you*.

1. **Wash** the chicken and **pat dry** with paper towels. **Measure** 1 tsp. of the oil, **drizzle** a bit on each breast, and **rub** to coat entirely. **Measure** ¼ tsp. of the salt, then **pinch** and **sprinkle** over the tops. **Season** the tops with ⅛ tsp. of the pepper (about 6 turns on a pepper mill). **Turn** the chicken over and **season** the same way with the remaining ¼ tsp. salt and ⅛ tsp. pepper. **Wash and dry** the thyme sprigs, then **pull** the leaves from their sprigs and **sprinkle** over the tops of the breasts Ⓐ.

Ⓐ　　　　　　　　　　　　　　　Ⓑ

2. **Place** your large skillet on the stove and **turn** the heat to medium. **Measure** and **pour** in the remaining 2 tsp. oil and **heat** until it shimmers (1 to 2 minutes). Using tongs, **add** the chicken, thyme-side down Ⓑ (you should hear a nice sizzle), and **cook** until the undersides are golden brown, 5 to 6 minutes. **Flip** the chicken (it should release easily from the pan) and continue to **cook** until golden brown and cooked through (you can **cut** into the thickest part to make sure it's no longer pink), 5 to 6 minutes more.

# SKILLET-ROASTED POTATOES & CHICKEN

A great one-pot meal. You will be working through a couple of steps (easy ones!) before you pop this little honey into the oven.

1 yellow onion
½ c. water
5 medium Yukon Gold
  potatoes (about 1¼ lbs.)
1 T. e.v. olive oil
2 T. fresh rosemary leaves
  (about 2 sprigs)
1½ tsp. kosher salt (1 tsp. +
  ½ tsp.)
¾ tsp. freshly ground black
  pepper (¼ tsp. + ½ tsp.)
4 small bone-in, skin-on
  chicken thighs (about
  1¼ lbs. total)
4 chicken drumsticks (about
  1 lb. total)
1 T. ground coriander

Tools needed: large
ovenproof skillet,
cutting board, chef's knife,
measuring spoons and
cups, paring knife, kitchen
timer.

* How-to:
  Slice an onion, p. 29

Don't Panic: Slicing an onion and a potato is hopefully no big thing for you at this point.

1. **Heat** the oven (with the oven rack in the low position) to 425°F. **Dust off** your large ovenproof skillet.

2. Thinly **slice** the onion * and **scatter** over the bottom of the skillet; **add** the water. **Wash** the potatoes (no need to peel) and **slice** them into about ¼-inch-thick rounds. **Lay** them over the onions, overlapping as necessary. **Drizzle** with the oil. **Wash** and dry the rosemary sprigs, then **pull** the leaves from their sprigs and **sprinkle** over the potatoes , along with 1 tsp. of the salt and ¼ tsp. of the pepper (about 12 turns on a pepper mill).

   Ⓐ

3. **Wash** the chicken and **pat dry** with paper towels. In a small bowl, **combine** the coriander and the remaining ½ tsp. salt and ½ tsp. pepper (about 24 turns on a pepper mill). Using your fingers, **rub** the spices into both sides of the chicken. **Lay** the chicken, skin side up, over the potatoes. **Roast** until the chicken is cooked through (you can cut into a piece to make sure it's no longer pink) and the potatoes are tender and can be easily pierced with the tip of a paring knife, about 1 hour.

# ROSEMARY CHICKEN UNDER A "BRICK"

This is my family's absolute favorite meal. It can be a bit messy on the stove, but is well worth it, I promise.

8 small bone-in, skin-on chicken thighs (about 2½ lbs.)

1 tsp. kosher salt (½ tsp. + ½ tsp.)

½ tsp. freshly ground black pepper (¼ tsp. + ¼ tsp.)

2 T. fresh rosemary leaves (about 2 sprigs)

2 tsp. e.v. olive oil

Tools needed: 2 large skillets, measuring spoons, tongs, kitchen timer, a "brick" (like a large can of tomatoes).

Don't Panic: You only need to have the patience to wait for the browning and crisping that occurs.

1. **Wash** the chicken and **pat dry** with paper towels. **Measure** ½ tsp. of the salt, then **pinch** and **sprinkle** over the tops. Then **season** the tops with ¼ tsp. of the pepper (about 12 turns on a pepper mill). **Turn** the chicken over and **season** the same way with the remaining ½ tsp. salt and ¼ tsp. pepper. **Wash** and dry the rosemary sprigs.

Ⓐ Ⓑ

2. **Place** your large skillet on the stove and **turn** the heat to medium-high. **Measure** and **pour** in the oil and **heat** until it shimmers (1 to 2 minutes). Using tongs, **place** all of the chicken skin side down in the skillet. **Pull** the rosemary leaves from their sprigs and **sprinkle** over the chicken Ⓐ. **Place** another skillet on top of the chicken and **weight** it down with something heavy (like a large can of tomatoes or perhaps you have a brick lying around your kitchen?). Ⓑ. **Set** the timer for 10 minutes.

3. **Lay** out a few paper towels on your counter. After 10 minutes, **lift** the weighted skillet off the chicken (onto the paper towels) so you can **check** if the chicken skin is a deep golden brown. It may need to cook 2 to 3 minutes more. Once the skin looks nice and brown, **flip** the chicken over. Again, **weight** it down with the skillet and continue to **cook** until cooked through (you can cut into a piece to make sure it's no longer pink), 3 to 5 minutes more.

# FAST & JUICY HERB-GRILLED CHICKEN

To make this recipe even easier, use the George Foreman grill.

4 boneless, skinless chicken
breasts (6 to 8 oz. each)
1 T. chopped fresh flat-leaf
parsley
1 T. chopped fresh thyme
1 T. chopped fresh rose-
mary
1 tsp. olive oil
½ tsp. kosher salt (¼ tsp. +
¼ tsp.)
¼ tsp. freshly ground black
pepper (⅛ tsp. + ⅛ tsp.)
1 lemon, cut into quarters

**Tools needed:** George
Foreman grill or panini
press, cutting board, chef's
knife, meat pounder or
rolling pin.

**\*How-to:**
Chop rosemary, thyme,
and parsley, pp. 32–33

**Don't Panic:** Pounding your
chicken to get it to an even
thickness is cathartic!

1. **Heat** a George Foreman grill
or panini press to medium-high
heat. **Wash** the chicken and
**pat dry** with paper towels. One
at a time, **place** the chicken
breasts in a ziptop bag and,
using a meat pounder or rolling
pin, **pound** to an even ½-inch
thickness **Ⓐ**. **Wash** and **chop**
the herbs\* and **combine** them.

**Ⓐ**

2. **Measure** the oil and **drizzle** a few drops on each breast. **Rub** to coat
entirely. **Measure** ¼ tsp. of the salt, then **pinch** and **sprinkle** over
the tops. Then **season** the tops with ⅛ tsp. of the pepper (about 6
turns on a pepper mill). **Turn** the chicken over and **season** the same
way with the remaining ¼ tsp. salt and ⅛ tsp. pepper.

3. **Sprinkle** both sides of the
chicken with the herbs **Ⓑ**. **Place**
the chicken in the grill (you may
be able to cook a few pieces at
once, depending on the size of
your grill) and **cook** until it's no
longer pink (cut into a piece to
make sure), about 3 minutes.
**Cut** the lemon into quarters and
**serve** with the chicken.

**Ⓑ**

# Sweet & Spicy Chicken Wings

These fly off the plate at our house (no pun intended). YES, even you can make your own wings and they will be SCRUMPTIOUS.

1½ tsp. freshly ground
   black pepper
2 T. dark brown sugar
2 tsp. sweet paprika
1½ tsp. kosher salt
1 tsp. ground cumin
2½ to 3 lbs. chicken wings
1 T. e.v. olive oil

Tools needed: small bowl, large bowl, measuring spoons, rimmed sheet pan, kitchen timer.

Don't Panic: Washing chicken may not be your thing. That's the only hard part.

1. **Heat** the oven (with the oven rack in the middle) to 425°F. In this recipe you become very intimate with your pepper mill. In a small bowl, **grind** the pepper (72 turns on a pepper mill—consider this your day's workout). Then **add** the brown sugar, paprika, salt, and cumin, and **combine**.

2. **Wash** the wings and **pat dry** with paper towels. In a large bowl, using your hands, **toss** together the wings and oil. **Sprinkle** in half of the spice rub, **toss** with your hands, then **sprinkle** in the rest and **toss** again Ⓐ. **Transfer** to a rimmed sheet pan and **arrange** in a single layer Ⓑ. **Roast** until the chicken is cooked through (you can cut into a wing to make sure it's no longer pink) and the skin is golden brown and crisp, 30 to 40 minutes.

Ⓐ

Ⓑ

# ROASTED CHICKEN DRUMSTICKS—4 EASY RECIPES!

Drumsticks deliver. It's an excellent, affordable, last-minute meal without a ton of dirty dishes. I'm giving you a variety of options. Most of these ingredients you may already have in your pantry.

### BARBECUE CHICKEN

8 chicken drumsticks
(about 2 lbs.)
¼ c. ketchup
2 T. low-sodium soy
sauce
1 T. dark brown sugar
1 tsp. hot chili sauce,
such as sriracha

### MUSTARD & ROSEMARY CHICKEN

8 chicken drumsticks
(about 2 lbs.)
¼ c. Dijon mustard
¼ c. fresh orange juice*
1 T. chopped fresh
rosemary (about
2 sprigs)*
2 tsp. e.v. olive oil
¼ tsp. kosher salt
¼ tsp. freshly ground
black pepper

### YOGURT & CUMIN CHICKEN

8 chicken drumsticks
(about 2 lbs.)
½ c. plain yogurt
2 cloves garlic,
chopped*
1 T. ground cumin
¾ tsp. kosher salt
½ tsp. cayenne pepper

### LEMON & SAGE CHICKEN

8 chicken drumsticks
(about 2 lbs.)
1 lemon, sliced into
8 very thin rounds
3 T. chopped fresh sage
(about 24 leaves)*
2 T. e.v. olive
¾ tsp. kosher salt
¼ tsp. freshly ground
black pepper

Tools needed: cutting board, chef's knife, small bowl, measuring cups and spoons, rimmed sheet pan, kitchen timer.

**\* How-to:**
Juice citrus, p. 25
Chop rosemary, p. 33
Chop garlic, p. 27
Chop sage, p. 32

**For each recipe:**

1. **Wash** the chicken and **pat dry** with paper towels. **Place** in a large ziptop bag and **open** the bag wide (you'll be adding the marinade to the bag).

2. In a small bowl, **combine** the ingredients for the marinade you desire. Then **add** to the bag of chicken. **Squeeze** out the air from the bag, **seal**, and **massage** to coat the chicken completely. If you have the time, let **marinate** (in the refrigerator) for at least 15 minutes and up to 24 hours.

3. **Heat** the oven (with the oven rack in the middle) to 425°F. **Arrange** the chicken in a single layer on a rimmed sheet pan and **roast** until cooked through (you can cut into one piece to make sure it's no longer pink), 35 to 40 minutes.

# Seriously Basic Roast Chicken

This is too easy and essential for the carnivore not to learn. It's the first recipe I teach my Can't Cook friends.

1 lemon
3 sprigs fresh rosemary
1 T. e.v. olive oil
1 tsp. kosher salt
½ tsp. freshly ground black pepper
1 whole chicken (4 lbs.)

Tools needed: cutting board, scissors, measuring spoons, paring knife, kitchen twine, large oven-proof skillet, kitchen timer, instant-read thermometer, chef's knife.

How-to carve? Go to: **tccb.co** Or, using your smartphone, scan the image on the left.

Don't Panic: Washing the chicken definitely freaks some people out, so be sure to keep paper towels handy for this recipe. Tying the legs together is easy. Carving is a fun adventure.

1. **Heat** the oven (with the oven rack in the middle) to 425°F.

2. Let's get everything ready before you touch the chicken: **wash** the lemon and **pierce** several times with the tip of a paring knife **Ⓐ**; **wash** the rosemary sprigs. **Set out** your oil, salt, and pepper. **Keep** paper towels handy.

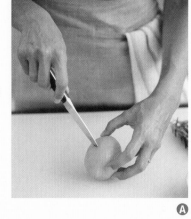

Ⓐ

3. **Remove** and **discard** the packet of giblets from the chicken. **Wash** the chicken inside and out and **pat dry** with paper towels. **Measure** the oil, then **drizzle** and **rub** it over the chicken. **Measure** the salt and pepper (about 24 turns on a pepper mill) and **sprinkle** on the chicken, inside and out. **Stuff** the lemon and whole rosemary sprigs into the cavity. **Snip** a forearm's length of kitchen twine and **tie** the legs together.

4. **Place** the chicken in the skillet and **transfer** to the oven (legs facing back). **Roast** until an instant-read thermometer reaches 165°F when inserted into the thickest part of the thigh, 50 to 60 minutes (**check** after 50 minutes). **Transfer** to a clean cutting board and **let rest** 5 to 10 minutes before carving. After it's carved, **reheat** the pan drippings and **drizzle** over the chicken.

# MEAT

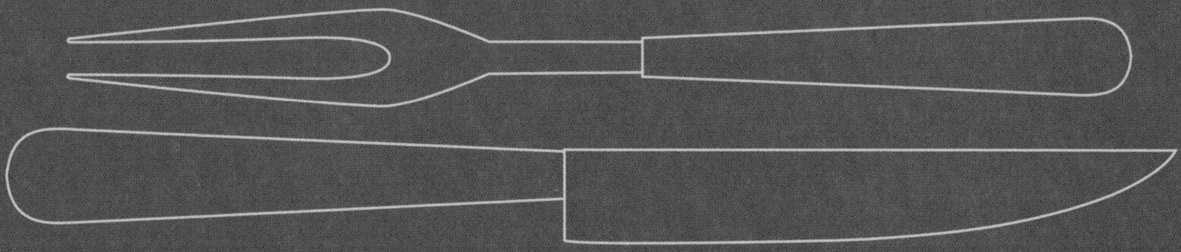

Simple Peppercorn Steak

**Herb-Roasted Beef with Potatoes & Carrots**

CHILI-RUBBED SKIRT STEAK TACOS

THE MOST SIMPLE, BROILED, PERFECT HAMBURGER

**Your First Chili**

**Bacon-Wrapped Meat Loaf**

PORK LOIN WITH APPLES & ONIONS

APPLE CIDER
PORK CHOPS

BROILED LAMB CHOPS

# Simple Peppercorn Steak

This steak is great. It has a nice kick, which is why I make it often, especially for my son Julian, whom we call "Little Tabasco."

2 New York strip steaks
   (about 1 inch thick, 1 lb.
   each)
1 T. whole black pepper-
   corns
2 tsp. canola oil
1 tsp. kosher salt (½ tsp. +
   ½ tsp.)

**Tools needed:** cutting
board, chef's knife,
small skillet, large skillet,
measuring spoons, tongs,
instant-read thermometer.

**\* How-to:**
   Crack black pepper, p. 38

**Don't Panic:** The key to cooking steak is learning when it's done to your liking, so I will guide you on this. I highly recommend purchasing an instant-read meat thermometer—it's an inexpensive and handy investment.

1. **Take** the steaks out of the refrigerator and let come to room temperature, about 20 minutes. Meanwhile, **crack** the pepper using the bottom of a small skillet until all of the peppercorns are cracked.**\***

2. If there is a lot of fat attached to the steak, **trim** it off with your chef's knife. **Drizzle** each steak with 1 tsp. of the oil and **rub** into both sides. **Measure** ½ tsp. of the salt, then **pinch** and **sprinkle** over the tops. **Turn** the steaks over and **season** the same way with the remaining ½ tsp. salt. **Rub** the cracked pepper into both sides.

3. **Place** a large skillet on the stove and **turn** the heat to medium-high. When the skillet is hot (after a minute or two), **add** the steaks. **Cook** the steaks on the first side until a deep brown crust has formed, 4 to 6 minutes. **Flip** the steaks and cook 4 to 6 minutes more for medium-rare, 125° to 130°F internal temperature. (To check the temperature of the steaks, **insert** an instant-read thermometer through the side to reach the center **Ⓐ**. **Check** the meat temperature chart on page 231, if need be, for desired doneness.) **Put** the meat back in the pan, and using your tongs, you can **hold** each steak on its side to sear the fat. **Transfer** the steaks to a cutting board and **let rest** 5 minutes before slicing.

**Ⓐ**

# Herb-Roasted Beef with Potatoes & Carrots

As far as a carnivore's dinner goes, what's better than juicy beef and minimal dish washing? This one-pan wonder will bring you a lifetime of dinners.

2 lbs. bottom round or
    rump roast
6 medium carrots (about
    1½ lbs.)
1 lb. baby red potatoes
    (about 12)
3 T. olive oil (2 T. + 1 T.)
1¼ tsp. kosher salt (½ tsp.
    + ¾ tsp.)
¾ tsp. freshly ground black
    pepper (¼ tsp. + ½ tsp.)
3 cloves garlic
1 T. dried Italian seasoning
    or oregano

Tools needed: cutting
board, chef's knife, rimmed
sheet pan, measuring
spoons, small bowl,
kitchen timer, instant-read
thermometer.

**\*** How-to:
    Cut carrots, p. 36
    Chop garlic, p. 27

Don't Panic: Cutting carrot sticks, chopping garlic, and using a meat thermometer may be new to you, but you've got all you need to figure it out.

1. **Heat** the oven (with the oven rack in the middle) to 375°F. **Take** the roast out of the refrigerator and let it come to room temperature, about 20 minutes.

2. Meanwhile, **peel** the carrots. **Cut** in half crosswise, then **cut** them into ½-inch-thick sticks.**\*** **Place** on a rimmed sheet pan. **Wash** the potatoes, **cut** them into quarters, and **add** to the pan. **Drizzle** with 2 T. of the oil, and **sprinkle** with ½ tsp. of the salt and ¼ tsp. of the pepper (about 12 turns on a pepper mill). **Toss** together with your hands and **spread** into a single layer.

3. **Place** the roast, fat side up, in the middle of the pan, pushing the vegetables aside so the roast sits directly on the pan.

4. **Chop** the garlic**\*** and **add** to a small bowl along with the Italian seasoning and the remaining 1 T. oil, ¾ tsp. salt, and ½ tsp. pepper (24 turns on a pepper mill). **Rub** evenly over the entire roast **Ⓐ**.

**Ⓐ**

5. **Roast** for about 1 hour for medium-rare (125° to 130°F internal temperature). After an hour, **insert** an instant-read thermometer into the center. **Check** the meat temperature chart on page 231 for desired doneness. **Let rest** 10 minutes before thinly slicing.

# THE MOST SIMPLE, BROILED, PERFECT HAMBURGER

Never made your own burger before? Broiling is the least messy way to do this, so fire up the heat. Let's get this done.

1½ lbs. ground chuck or sirloin (85% to 90% lean)
½ tsp. kosher salt (¼ tsp. + ¼ tsp.)
¼ tsp. freshly ground black pepper (⅛ tsp. + ⅛ tsp.)
4 hamburger buns
Your favorite toppings

**Tools needed:** broiler pan or rimmed sheet pan, measuring spoons, metal spatula, kitchen timer.

**Don't Panic:** Shaping the meat patties and broiling to the perfect temperature might even be exciting for you.

1. It's time to touch raw meat. First, **divide** into 4 even pieces. **Shape** into 4 balls, then gently **press** each into a ¾-inch-thick patty—be sure not to overhandle/squeeze/smash it because it will toughen. Slightly **flatten** each patty a little more in the middle **Ⓐ** (they tend to plump in the middle as they cook). If the edges crack, **press** them back together.

Ⓐ

2. **Measure** ¼ tsp. of the salt, then **pinch** and **sprinkle** over the tops. Then **season** the tops with ⅛ tsp. of the pepper (about 6 turns on a pepper mill). **Turn** the patties over and **season** the same way with the remaining ¼ tsp. salt and ⅛ tsp. pepper. **Refrigerate** on a plate until you're ready to cook.

3. **Get** your toppings ready.

4. **Heat** the broiler (with the oven rack about 4 inches from the top). **Place** your patties on a broiler pan or rimmed sheet pan and **slide** under the broiler. **Keep** a close eye on them and **cook** until browned on the first side, 3 to 5 minutes. Then **flip** (resist the urge to smash down on the patties with your spatula) and **cook** another 3 to 4 minutes for medium. **Transfer** to a plate to rest.

5. To heat the buns, **split** them open and **place** cut side up on a rimmed sheet pan and **heat** under the broiler. **Build** your burger.

# Your First Chili

DO NOT BE ALARMED. This ingredient list is long, I know, I know! Most of the ingredients you may already have in your pantry. You can measure and pour, right? That's the bulk of the work, I promise.

1 can (28 oz.) diced tomatoes

2 cans (15 oz. each) kidney beans

1 yellow onion

1 bell pepper

1 T. e.v. olive oil

1 pound ground chuck or sirloin (85% to 90% lean)

3 T. chili powder

1 tsp. ground cumin

½ tsp. chipotle chile powder

2 T. tomato paste

1 T. cider vinegar or red wine vinegar

1 T. dark brown sugar

1½ tsp. kosher salt

¼ tsp. freshly ground black pepper

1 c. water

Your favorite toppings

Tools needed: cutting board, chef's knife, measuring cups and spoons, wooden spoon, can opener, large pot, strainer, kitchen timer.

*How-to:
  Chop an onion, p. 29

Don't Panic: Chopping an onion and bell pepper is the only thing you need to do with your knife. The rest is very easy.

1. **Open** the can of tomatoes and **drain** and **rinse** the beans.

2. **Chop** the onion and **push** to one side of the cutting board.* **Cut** the bell pepper into 1-inch pieces. To do this, first **cut** into quarters from stem to bottom, then **cut out** and **discard** the seeds and white part. **Cut** each piece in half again, then **cut** crosswise into 1-inch pieces.

3. **Place** a large pot (5- to 6-qt.) on the stove and **turn** the heat to medium-high.

4. **Measure** and **pour** in the oil and **heat** until it shimmers (1 to 2 minutes). **Add** the onion and bell pepper and **cook,** stirring often, until softened, 5 to 6 minutes. **Add** the meat and **cook,** breaking it up with a wooden spoon, until browned and cooked through, 6 to 8 minutes.

5. **Set up** your dry ingredients by the stove. **Stir** in the chili powder, cumin, and chipotle powder and **cook,** stirring, for 1 minute. **Add** the tomato paste. **Stir** in the tomatoes, vinegar, brown sugar, salt, and pepper (about 12 turns on a pepper mill). **Add** the beans to the pot along with the water and let come to a boil. **Lower** the heat to medium-low and **simmer** (low boil), stirring occasionally, for at least 20 minutes to develop the flavors (you may have to lower the heat if it starts to boil too rapidly).

6. If the chili becomes too thick, you can **add** up to ½ c. more water. **Serve** as is or with your favorite toppings, like grated Cheddar, sour cream, and chopped red onion.

# Bacon-Wrapped Meat Loaf

I top this ol'-timer with bacon. Its crispy bits and smoky flavor are enough to drive a man (or lady) wild.

Cooking spray
½ of a 10-oz. box frozen chopped spinach
¼ c. low-fat or whole milk
¼ c. dried bread crumbs
2 large eggs
1 small yellow onion
1¼ lbs. ground chuck or sirloin (85% to 90% lean)
½ c. grated Parmesan
½ tsp. garlic powder
½ tsp. onion powder
½ tsp. kosher salt
½ tsp. freshly ground black pepper
5 strips bacon

Tools needed: 8½ x 4½-inch loaf pan, strainer, cutting board, chef's knife, food processor (optional), measuring cups and spoons, cheese grater (if grating it yourself), small bowl, large bowl, fork, kitchen timer, instant-read thermometer.

* How-to:
   Chop an onion, p. 29

Don't Panic: Chopping an onion and getting your hands dirty mixing the meat might scare you, but I bet you've faced more adversity than this in your lifetime.

1. **Heat** the oven (with the oven rack in the middle) to 400°F. **Coat** the inside of an 8½ x 4½-inch loaf pan with cooking spray. To thaw the spinach, **place** in a strainer and **pass** under hot running water until thawed, then **squeeze** out all of the excess water. In a small bowl, **combine** the milk and bread crumbs and **set aside** for a few minutes to soften.

2. **Crack** the eggs into a large bowl and **beat** with a fork. **Chop** the onion * (you can also use a food processor for this) and **add** it to the eggs. **Add** the meat, Parmesan, garlic and onion powders, salt, and pepper (about 24 turns on a pepper mill). **Add** the milk-soaked bread crumbs and thawed spinach. Using your hands, gently **mix** all the ingredients until well combined.

3. **Place** the meat mixture in the prepared pan and gently **press** in. **Zigzag** the bacon strips over the top to cover completely Ⓐ. **Bake** until an instant-read thermometer inserted into the center reads 160°F (check the temperature after 55 minutes), 55 to 60 minutes. **Remove** from the oven and **let rest** for 5 minutes before lifting from the pan and slicing.

Ⓐ

# APPLE CIDER PORK CHOPS

Making a sauce is completely intimidating, right? Not this one. It's made from one ingredient—apple cider. And you don't even *know* you are making a sauce—it just happens magically.

4 boneless pork chops
   (1 inch thick, about
   1½ lbs. total)
1 tsp. kosher salt (½ tsp. +
   ½ tsp.)
¼ tsp. freshly ground black
   pepper (⅛ tsp. + ⅛ tsp.)
2 tsp. e.v. olive oil
½ c. apple cider

Tools needed: measuring cups and spoons, large skillet, tongs, instant-read thermometer, wooden spoon.

Don't Panic: You've got only two things to keep in the back of your mind: making sure the pork is done and letting the apple cider simmer long enough to turn into sauce.

1. **Take** the pork out of the refrigerator and let it come to room temperature, about 15 minutes.

2. **Measure** ½ tsp. of the salt, then **pinch** and **sprinkle** over the tops of the pork. Then **season** with ⅛ tsp. of the pepper (about 6 turns on a pepper mill). **Turn** the pork over and **season** the same way with the remaining ½ tsp. salt and ⅛ tsp. pepper.

3. **Place** your large skillet on the stove and **turn** the heat to medium. **Measure** and **pour** in the oil and **heat** until it shimmers (1 to 2 minutes). Using tongs, **add** the pork (you should hear a gratifying sizzle). **Cook** until the undersides are golden brown, 5 to 6 minutes. Using tongs, **flip** (they should release easily from the pan) and continue to **cook** until an instant-read thermometer inserted into the center through the side reads 145°F, 5 to 6 minutes more. **Use** your tongs to **hold** each chop on its side to **sear** the fat.

4. **Transfer** the pork to plates. **Measure** and **pour** the apple cider into the skillet and **return** it to medium-high heat. Using a wooden spoon, **scrape** up the yummy browned bits from the bottom of the pan Ⓐ. Let the cider simmer (low boil) for 2 to 3 minutes to thicken it just slightly. **Spoon** it over the pork chops.

Ⓐ

# BROILED LAMB CHOPS WITH MINT JELLY

Look at how few ingredients are needed here! You can do this. Buy yourself a nice mint jelly at a better grocery store.

8 small loin lamb chops
   (about 1 inch thick)
¾ tsp. kosher salt
¼ tsp. freshly ground black
   pepper
Your favorite mint jelly

Tools needed: rimmed sheet pan, measuring spoons, tongs, kitchen timer, instant-read thermometer.

Don't Panic: Broiling might scare you. All you need to do is check your timer and stick your head in the oven (but not completely) to check on what's happening.

1. **Take** the lamb out of the refrigerator and let it come to room temperature, about 15 minutes.

2. **Heat** the broiler (with the oven rack about 4 inches from the top).

3. **Measure** the salt, then **pinch** and **sprinkle** about half of it evenly over the tops of the lamb. **Turn** the lamb over and **sprinkle** with the remaining salt. Then **season** both sides with the pepper (about 6 turns on a pepper mill per side).

4. **Place** the lamb on a rimmed sheet pan. **Transfer** to the oven and **broil** 4 to 5 minutes on the first side. Now, remember—broiling happens very quickly. Keep your eye on these. **Flip** the lamb and **broil** 3 to 4 minutes more for medium-rare (125° to 130°F internal temperature). To check the internal temperature, **insert** an instant-read thermometer through the side to reach the center without touching the bone. **Check** the meat temperature chart on page 231, if need be, for desired doneness. **Serve** with mint jelly.

# F🐟SH

ROASTED STRIPED BASS & TOMATOES

Succulent Lemon-Thyme Salmon

Bread Crumb Bass

Perfect Halibut over Spinach

**Hoisin Halibut**

CRISPY SHRIMP

STEWY SHRIMP WITH TOMATOES & WHITE BEANS

# ROASTED STRIPED BASS & TOMATOES

Soooo elegant and delicious! What's more, there is no easier way to cook a piece of fish. This is a great first step out of Can't Cooksville in the fish category.

2 pints grape tomatoes

8 sprigs thyme

4 cloves garlic

2 T. plus 1 tsp. e.v. olive oil

1 tsp. kosher salt (½ tsp. + ½ tsp.)

¼ tsp. freshly ground black pepper (⅛ tsp. + ⅛ tsp.)

4 pieces striped bass, salmon, or halibut fillet (6 oz. each, about 1 inch thick)

Tools needed: cutting board, chef's knife, rimmed sheet pan, measuring spoons, kitchen timer, paring knife.

*How-to:

Smash and peel garlic, pp. 26-27

Check when fish is done, p. 41

Don't Panic: Smashing the garlic could bring you joy. Taking the fish out of the oven at the right time is a "moment," but it's easily explained for you on p. 41.

1. **Heat** the oven (with the oven rack in the middle) to 425°F. **Wash** the tomatoes and thyme sprigs and **place** in a rimmed sheet pan. **Smash** and **peel** the garlic* and **add** to the pan along with 2 T. of the oil, ½ tsp. of the salt, and ⅛ tsp. of the pepper (about 6 turns on a pepper mill). **Toss** everything together with your hands .

2. **Wash** the fish and **pat dry** with paper towels. **Place** in the middle of the pan, pushing the tomatoes aside as you need to. **Measure** the remaining 1 tsp. oil and **drizzle** a few drops over the top of each piece of fish and **rub** to coat . **Measure** the remaining ½ tsp. salt, then **pinch** and **sprinkle** over the tops. Then **season** the tops with the remaining ⅛ tsp. pepper (about 6 turns on a pepper mill).

3. **Roast** until the fish flakes easily when pierced with the tip of a paring knife* and the tomatoes are softened, 18 to 22 minutes.

# Succulent Lemon-Thyme Salmon

Tackle this. You'll make this meal over and over again.

3 lemons

24 sprigs thyme

4 pieces skinless salmon
   fillet (6 oz. each)

1 tsp. e.v. olive oil

½ tsp. kosher salt

⅛ tsp. freshly ground black
   pepper

**Tools needed:** rimmed
sheet pan, cutting board,
chef's knife, measuring
spoons, kitchen timer,
paring knife.

**\*How-to:**
   Check when fish is done,
      p. 41

**Don't Panic:** Using your broiler is up there in the "this is scary"
department—let's fix that.

1. **Heat** the broiler (with the oven rack about 4 inches from the top).

2. **Wash** the lemons. **Cut off** the
   ends from 2 of the lemons.
   **Slice** those 2 lemons into
   rounds—try to get 6 slices per
   lemon. **Arrange** the 12 slices
   on your rimmed sheet pan in
   4 rows of 3. **Wash** and **dry** the
   thyme sprigs. **Top** each row
   with 6 sprigs .

3. **Wash** the salmon and **pat dry**
   with paper towels. **Lay** the
   salmon on each lemon-thyme
   bed, tucking the thyme under
   the salmon so it doesn't burn.
   **Measure, drizzle,** and **rub** the tops of the salmon with oil (¼ tsp.
   per piece). **Measure** the salt, then **pinch** and **sprinkle** over the
   tops. Then **season** the tops with the pepper (about 6 turns on a
   pepper mill).

**Ⓐ**

4. **Slide** the pan under the broiler. **Set** the timer for 5 minutes. After
   5 minutes, **pull** the pan out to **check** the fish for doneness: you
   want the tops of the salmon to be golden brown. To **check** the
   inside: the salmon should flake easily when pierced with the tip of
   a paring knife.**\*** If you would like to cook it longer, it can go back
   in the oven for 2 to 5 minutes more, depending on the thickness
   of the salmon and the strength of your broiler. **Cut** the extra lemon
   into wedges and **serve** with the salmon, for squeezing.

111

# Bread Crumb Bass

You only break out the knife once, so my most beginner friends worship this recipe. You can accomplish this one.

6 medium shallots
2 T. e.v. olive oil (1 T. + 1 T.)
4 pieces skinless striped
   bass, fluke, or tilapia
   (6 oz. each)
¼ c. dried bread crumbs
1 tsp. dried oregano
¼ tsp. kosher salt
¼ tsp. freshly ground black
   pepper

**Tools needed:** cutting board, paring knife, rimmed sheet pan, measuring cups and spoons, small bowl, paring knife, kitchen timer.

**\*** How-to:
   Slice a shallot, p. 30
   Check when fish is done,
      p. 41

**Don't Panic:** Peeling and slicing the shallots is no problem for you.

1. **Heat** the oven (with the oven rack in the middle) to 400°F. **Cut off** the stem end of each shallot and **peel.** Thinly **slice** the shallots into rounds and **separate** into rings (I promise this is the hardest part!).**\*** **Transfer** to a rimmed sheet pan and **drizzle** with 1 T. of the oil. **Toss** with your hands and **arrange** in a single layer.

2. **Wash** the fish and **pat dry** with paper towels. **Place** on top of the shallots.

3. In a small bowl, **combine** the bread crumbs, oregano, salt, pepper (about 12 turns on a pepper mill), and the remaining 1 T. oil. **Sprinkle** and pat about 1 T. of the crumbs over each piece of fish . **Transfer** to the oven and **bake.** You know it's done when the fish flakes easily when pierced with the tip of a paring knife,**\*** the bread crumbs are golden brown, and the shallots are tender, 15 to 20 minutes. If you are using fluke or tilapia, bake for 12 to 15 minutes. **Serve** the fish over the shallots.

Ⓐ

# Perfect Halibut over Spinach

You get your side dish and your main course made at the same time. Light, delicious, and also great for you. Love. It.

1 clove garlic

10 oz. fresh baby spinach
(about 12 packed c.)

1 T. plus ½ tsp. e.v. olive oil

¾ tsp. kosher salt (¼ tsp. +
½ tsp.)

4 skinless halibut fillets
(6 oz. each, about 1 inch
thick)

1 lemon

**Tools needed:** large
bowl, cutting board, salad
spinner, measuring spoons,
chef's knife, rimmed sheet
pan, kitchen timer, paring
knife.

**\*How-to:**
Smash and peel garlic,
pp. 26–27
Check when fish is done,
p. 41

**Don't Panic:** Checking for doneness and smashing garlic are two things in your wheelhouse.

1. **Heat** the oven (with the oven rack in the middle) to 425°F. **Smash** and **peel** the garlic \* and **rub** a rimmed sheet pan with it, then **discard. Put** the spinach in a salad spinner, **wash,** and **spin** dry. **Transfer** to a large bowl and **toss** with 1 T. of the oil and ¼ tsp. of the salt. **Spread** evenly on the pan.

2. **Wash** the halibut and **pat dry** with paper towels. **Drizzle** the remaining ½ tsp. oil over the fish (⅛ tsp. over each piece) and **rub** to coat both sides. **Measure** the remaining ½ tsp. salt, then **pinch** and **sprinkle** over the tops. **Place** on top of the spinach.

3. **Wash** the lemon. **Cut off** the ends and **slice** the lemon into 8 rounds. **Top** the fish with 2 lemon rounds each Ⓐ. **Bake** until the halibut flakes easily when pierced with the tip of a paring knife, 10 to 15 minutes.\* **Serve** with the spinach.

Ⓐ

# Hoisin Halibut

I can get anyone to eat anything in my house if it's made with hoisin sauce. This sweet and tasty condiment is easily found in any general grocery store.

¼ c. hoisin sauce

1 T. low-sodium soy sauce

8 scallions

1 T. e.v. olive oil

4 pieces skinless halibut
   fillet (6 oz. each, about
   1 inch thick)

Tools needed: cutting board, paring knife, small bowl, measuring cups and spoons, large baking dish, aluminum foil, kitchen timer.

\* How-to:
   Trim scallions, p. 31
   Check when fish is done,
      p. 41

Don't Panic: To check for doneness, you know by now to stick the tip of your paring knife in lightly to see if the fish flakes easily.

1. **Heat** the oven (with the oven rack in the middle) to 425°F.

2. In a small bowl, **combine** the hoisin and soy sauce.

3. **Cut off** the roots from the scallions and **peel** off the outer membrane.\* **Wash. Cut off** and **discard** about 2 inches from the dark green tops. **Use** the tip of your paring knife to **cut** the scallions down the middle lengthwise Ⓐ. **Place** in a large baking dish. **Drizzle** with the oil and **toss** to coat evenly. **Arrange** in a single layer.

Ⓐ

4. **Wash** the halibut and **pat dry** with paper towels. **Place** the halibut on top of the scallions. **Spoon** and **spread** the sauce evenly over each piece Ⓑ. **Cover** the dish with foil so it's airtight. **Bake** until the halibut flakes easily when pierced with the tip of a paring knife, 10 to 15 minutes.\* **Serve** with the scallions.

Ⓑ

# CRISPY SHRIMP

These get eaten the minute they hit the table at my house. It's similar to scampi but way easier and more healthful. Don't pass this one by (unless you don't like shrimp).

1 lb. (about 20) large shrimp (thawed if frozen; see p. 233)

¾ c. panko (Japanese-style) bread crumbs

2 T. e.v. olive oil

1 tsp. dried oregano

½ tsp. smoked or sweet paprika

½ tsp. kosher salt

¼ tsp. freshly ground black pepper

1 lime, quartered

**Tools needed:** measuring cups and spoons, large bowl, rimmed sheet pan, kitchen timer.

**\*** How-to:
Peel and devein shrimp, p. 40

**Don't Panic:** Peeling the shrimp takes a couple of minutes. If you don't want to do this, buy them already peeled and deveined (but be aware that it's a little more expensive that way).

1. **Heat** the oven (with the oven rack in the middle) to 400°F. **Peel** and **devein** the shrimp if the shell is on; leave on the tails.**\*** **Rinse** the shrimp, making sure that the dark line (the vein) is removed.

2. In a large bowl, **combine** the panko, oil, oregano, paprika, salt, and pepper (about 12 turns on a pepper mill). **Add** the shrimp to the bowl and **toss** to coat, pressing the bread crumbs to help them adhere to the shrimp. Try to use one hand so you have a free, clean hand just in case . . . **A**.

3. **Place** the shrimp in a single layer on a rimmed sheet pan and **sprinkle** with any extra bread crumbs that are left in the bowl. **Bake** until the bread crumbs are crispy and the shrimp is cooked through (you can cut into one to make sure), 12 to 15 minutes. **Serve** with the quartered lime for squeezing.

**A**

119

# STEWY SHRIMP WITH TOMATOES & WHITE BEANS

Okay, beginners. Do this one. The result feels fancy, but the process is completely doable—even for my most fearful friends.

4 slices French bread
  (½ inch thick)
4 T. e.v. olive oil (2 T. + 2 T.)
2 c. arugula
3 cloves garlic
1 can (15 oz.) diced
  tomatoes
1 can (15 oz.) cannellini
  beans, drained and rinsed
½ c. dry white wine, such as
  sauvignon blanc
1½ lbs. (about 30) large
  shrimp (thawed if frozen;
  see p. 233)
¼ tsp. crushed red pepper
⅛ tsp. freshly ground black
  pepper
Kosher salt, to taste

Tools needed: small bowl,
pastry brush, rimmed sheet
pan, salad spinner, strainer,
can opener, measuring
cups and spoons, chef's
knife, paring knife, cutting
board, large pot, wooden
spoon, tongs.

**\* How-to:**
  Chop garlic, p. 27
  Peel and devein shrimp,
    p. 40
  Season to taste, p. 39

Don't Panic: Chopping garlic as well as peeling shrimp may scare you. Find the strength.

1. **Heat** the broiler (with the oven rack about 4 inches from the top). **Brush** both sides of the bread slices with 2 T. of the oil and place on a rimmed sheet pan. **Broil** until toasted, 1 to 2 minutes per side. **Set aside.**

2. Being organized is the key to your success here. **Wash** the arugula and **spin** dry. **Chop** your garlic.**\*** **Open** the can of tomatoes, **drain** and **rinse** the beans, and **measure** the wine. **Peel** and **devein** the shrimp if the shell is on and **rinse**, making sure that the dark line (the vein) is removed.**\*** **Put** everything near your stovetop.

3. **Place** a large pot (5- to 6-qt.) on the stove and **turn** the heat to medium. **Measure** and **pour** in the remaining 2 T. oil and **heat** until it shimmers (1 to 2 minutes). **Add** the garlic and **cook** until fragrant (do not let it brown), about 30 seconds. **Add** the tomatoes and **cook,** stirring, for 2 minutes. **Pour** in the wine and bring to a low boil. **Add** the shrimp and **cook,** turning occasionally with tongs, until opaque throughout, 3 to 5 minutes Ⓐ.

4. **Stir** in the beans, arugula, red pepper, and black pepper (6 turns on a pepper mill) and **cook,** stirring often, until the beans are heated through and the arugula is just wilted, about 2 minutes. **Season** with salt to taste.**\*** **Serve** with the toasted bread.

Ⓐ

121

# PASTA & PIZZA

SWEET CHERRY TOMATO PASTA

FREAKY GREEK PASTA

**Turkey Bolognese**

**Baked Egg Noodles & Cheese**

Spaghetti Marinara

**SLOW-COOKER LASAGNA**

**Cacio e Pepe**

**Slammin' Pasta with Clams**

Pesto Pasta

PIZZA MARGHERITA

# SWEET CHERRY TOMATO PASTA

This is a home run for pasta lovers. There's nothing tricky here. It's on permanent rotation at my house.

2 cloves garlic

1 c. loosely packed
   fresh basil leaves, plus
   12 leaves

1½ lbs. cherry tomatoes

3 T. e.v. olive oil (2 T. + 1 T.)

2 T. water

1 tsp. kosher salt

¼ tsp. freshly ground black
   pepper, plus more for
   serving

1 box (1 lb.) whole wheat
   or regular spaghetti

1 c. whole milk or part-skim
   ricotta cheese

Tools needed: 2 large
pots (1 lid), colander,
cutting board, chef's knife,
salad spinner, kitchen timer,
tongs, measuring cups and
spoons, wooden spoon.

*How-to:
   Chop garlic, p. 27.

*Pasta is al dente
when it still has a
little firmness when
you bite into it. It
should not be mushy.*

Don't Panic: Chopping garlic is in our How-to. You can, and will, make this again and again.

1. **Fill** a large pot with water (to about 1 inch from the top). **Place** on the stove and **turn** the heat to high to bring to a boil. **Place** a colander in the sink. **Chop** the garlic.* **Measure** the 1 c. basil, **wash** it, **dry** it, and **tear** it. **Wash** and **dry** the 12 basil leaves. **Wash** the tomatoes. **Place** your ingredients near the stove along with your timer.

2. **Place** another large pot on the stove and **turn** the heat to medium. **Measure** and **pour** in 2 T. of the oil and **heat** until it shimmers (1 to 2 minutes). **Scoop** up the chopped garlic with your knife Ⓐ and **add** to the pot, then **add** the 1 c. torn basil leaves. **Cook**, stirring with a wooden spoon, for 30 seconds, until fragrant. **Stir** in the tomatoes and water along with the salt and pepper (about 12 turns on a pepper mill). **Cover** and **cook** for 8 minutes. **Uncover** and continue to **cook**, stirring, until the tomatoes start to break apart and release their juices.

Ⓐ

3. When the water comes to a boil, **add** the pasta and **cook** according to the package directions. Once the pasta is al dente, **drain** it into the colander, then **add** it to the pot with the tomatoes. **Add** the ricotta, 12 basil leaves, a few extra turns on the pepper mill, and the remaining 1 T. oil. **Toss** and **serve**.

# FREAKY GREEK PASTA

You will definitely give the impression that you are a really freaking good cook if you serve this to the people in your life. The crunchy almonds are a delight.

1 bunch broccoli
8 oz. feta (2 c., crumbled)
1 lemon
½ tsp. dried oregano
¼ tsp. crushed red pepper
¼ tsp. freshly ground black
   pepper
½ c. sliced almonds
1 box (1 lb.) whole wheat
   or regular penne
2 T. e.v. olive oil
Kosher salt, to taste

Tools needed: large pot,
colander, cutting board,
chef's knife, strainer,
very large bowl, grater/
zester, measuring cups
and spoons, small skillet,
kitchen timer.

* How-to:
   Zest citrus, p. 24
   Toast sliced almonds,
      p. 37
   Season to taste, p. 39

Don't Panic: Toasting the almonds, cutting the broccoli into florets, and grating the lemon zest are all easy things to learn.

1. **Fill** a large pot with water (to about 1 inch from the top). **Place** on the stove and **turn** the heat to high to bring to a boil. **Place** a colander in the sink.

2. Meanwhile, **cut** the broccoli into small florets, leaving a little bit of stalk attached. **Place** in a strainer, and **pass** under cold running water to wash. **Drain** the feta (if in water) and **crumble** (about 2 c.) into a very large bowl. **Wash** and **dry** the outside of the lemon and **grate** the zest directly into the bowl.* **Add** the oregano, red pepper, and black pepper (about 12 turns on a pepper mill).

3. **Place** a small skillet on the stove and **add** the almonds. **Turn** the heat to medium. **Stir** or **shake** the almonds often (so they cook evenly), until toasted and fragrant, 3 to 5 minutes.* **Remove** from the heat.

4. When the water comes to a boil, **add** the pasta. **Set** the timer for 3 minutes less than the package directions call for. When the timer goes off, **add** the broccoli to the pot and **cook** together until the broccoli is tender and the pasta is al dente, 3 minutes more. **Drain** everything into the colander and **add** immediately to the large bowl. **Sprinkle** in the toasted almonds and **combine** with the ingredients on the bottom. **Drizzle** in the oil and **toss** once or twice more. **Season** with salt to taste.*

# Turkey Bolognese

Use the food processor to chop the vegetables so you don't spend a lot of time with a knife.

1 yellow onion

2 medium carrots

4 cloves garlic

2 T. e.v. olive oil

1¼ tsp. kosher salt (½ tsp. + ¾ tsp.)

½ c. dry white wine, such as sauvignon blanc

1 can (28 oz.) crushed tomatoes

1 lb. ground turkey

1 tsp. dried oregano

¼ tsp. crushed red pepper

¼ tsp. freshly ground black pepper

¼ c. chopped fresh flat-leaf parsley

1 box (1 lb.) whole wheat or regular fettuccine

Grated Parmesan, for serving

Tools needed: 2 large pots, colander, cutting board, chef's knife, food processor, measuring cups and spoons, wooden spoon, can opener, cheese grater (if grating it yourself), kitchen timer.

**\*** How-to:

Use a food processor, p. 16

Smash and peel garlic, pp. 26–27

Chop parsley, pp. 32-33

Don't Panic: Learn how to use the food processor, because this recipe is worth it (and it takes away the bulk of the work).

1. **Fill** a large pot with water (to about 1 inch from the top). **Place** on the stove and **turn** the heat to high to bring to a boil. **Place** a colander in the sink.

2. Meanwhile, **chop** the onion, carrots, and garlic in the food processor**\*** (or by hand, by all means!). To use the processor, first **peel**, then **quarter** the onion and carrots; **smash** and **peel** the garlic.**\*** **Put** in the processor and **pulse** several times until chopped.

3. **Place** another large pot on the stove and **turn** the heat to medium-high. **Measure** and **pour** in the oil and **heat** until it shimmers (1 to 2 minutes). **Add** the chopped vegetables and ½ tsp. of the salt and **cook**, stirring often with a wooden spoon, until softened, 5 to 6 minutes. Meanwhile, **measure** the wine and **open** the can of tomatoes. **Place** them and your spices near the stove.

4. **Add** the wine to the vegetables and **stir** until it evaporates, about 1 minute. **Add** the turkey and **cook**, breaking it up with a wooden spoon, until no longer pink, 5 to 6 minutes. **Add** the tomatoes, oregano, red pepper, black pepper (about 12 turns on a pepper mill), and the remaining ¾ tsp. salt. **Lower** the heat to medium-low and simmer (low boil), stirring occasionally, for 10 minutes. **Wash** the parsley, then **chop** it **\*** by hand and **stir** it into the sauce.

5. When the water comes to a boil, **add** the pasta and **cook** according to the package directions. Once the pasta is al dente, **drain** it into the colander and **divide** among bowls. **Top** with the sauce and **sprinkle** with Parmesan.

# Baked Egg Noodles & Cheese

This is really, really easy macaroni and cheese. The higher the quality of the cheese you use, the better. Try not to eat the entire batch before serving.

Cooking spray
1½ c. grated sharp white Cheddar (6 oz.)
1½ c. grated sharp yellow Cheddar (6 oz.)
¾ c. 1% or 2% milk
½ c. reduced-fat sour cream
2 large eggs
1 bag (1 lb.) wide egg noodles
¼ c. dried bread crumbs

Tools needed: large pot, colander, 2½-qt. baking dish, cheese grater, medium bowl, large bowl, measuring cups, whisk, kitchen timer, silicone spatula.

Don't Panic: Using a cheese grater is awkward, I know. We'll get through this.

1. **Heat** the oven (with the oven rack in the middle) to 425°F. **Fill** a large pot with water (to about 1 inch from the top). **Place** on the stove and **turn** the heat to high to bring to a boil. **Place** a colander in the sink. **Coat** the inside of a 2½-qt. baking dish with cooking spray.

2. **Grate** the cheeses , **place** in a medium bowl, and **mix** together. (Protect your knuckles: Stop grating before the cheese block gets too small. Chop into smaller pieces with a knife instead.) In a large bowl, **whisk** together the milk, sour cream, and eggs.

3. When the water comes to a boil, **add** the noodles and **cook** for 3 minutes. **Drain** into the colander and **pass** under cold running water to stop the cooking. **Add** the noodles to the large bowl with the sour cream mixture and **stir. Add** 2 c. of the grated cheese to the noodles and **mix** well. Using a silicone spatula, **pour** and **scrape** into the prepared baking dish. **Add** the bread crumbs to the remaining 1 c. cheese and **toss** together with your hands, then **sprinkle** over the top of the noodles. **Bake** until golden brown and crispy on top, 15 to 20 minutes.

Ⓐ

# Spaghetti Marinara

With just a few ingredients and only a small bit of time, you've got a homemade marinara you can brag about. It will be seriously cool if you learn how to do this.

1 can (28 oz.) crushed tomatoes
3 cloves garlic
2 T. e.v. olive oil
½ tsp. kosher salt
¼ tsp. crushed red pepper
¼ tsp. freshly ground black pepper
1 box (1 lb.) whole wheat or regular spaghetti
Grated Parmesan, for serving

Tools needed: large pot, colander, cutting board, chef's knife, measuring spoons, large saucepan, wooden spoon, can opener, cheese grater (if grating it yourself), kitchen timer.

*How-to:
Chop garlic, p. 27

Don't Panic: Chopping the garlic is easy breezy.

1. **Fill** a large pot with water (to about 1 inch from the top). **Place** on the stove and **turn** the heat to high to bring to a boil. **Place** a colander in the sink. **Open** the can of tomatoes.

2. **Chop** the garlic.*

3. **Place** a large saucepan on the stove and **turn** the heat to medium. **Measure** and **pour** in the oil and **heat** until it shimmers (1 to 2 minutes). **Scoop** up the chopped garlic with your knife and **add** to the pot. **Cook**, stirring with a wooden spoon, until light golden brown, about 1 minute . **Remove** the pan from the heat and **add** the tomatoes. Then **stir** in the salt, red pepper, and black pepper (12 turns on a pepper mill). **Return** to the heat and let come to a boil, then **lower** the heat to medium-low and **simmer** (low boil), stirring often, for 15 minutes. If the sauce becomes too thick and starts to sputter, **add** up to ½ c. water for desired consistency.

4. When the water comes to a boil, **add** the pasta and **cook** according to the package directions. Once the pasta is al dente, **drain** it into the colander. **Divide** the pasta among bowls and **top** with the marinara. **Serve** with grated Parmesan.

133

# Slow-Cooker Lasagna

I first featured this recipe on *Oprah*. The response from beginners to cooking whizzes alike was extraordinary. Give it a whirl.

4 cloves garlic

2 cans (28 oz. each)
    crushed tomatoes

2 T. dried oregano

½ tsp. kosher salt

¼ tsp. crushed red pepper

¼ tsp. freshly ground black
    pepper

2 containers (15 oz. each)
    whole milk or part-skim
    ricotta cheese

2 c. (8 oz.) grated
    mozzarella (1 c. + 1 c.)

¼ c. grated Parmesan

5 oz. fresh baby spinach
    (about 6 packed c.)

16 lasagna noodles (about
    ¾ of a 1-lb. box)

Tools needed: 5- to 6-qt.
slow cooker, 2 medium
bowls, cutting board, chef's
knife, cheese grater (if
grating it yourself), salad
spinner, measuring cups
and spoons, 2 spoons,
paring knife.

\* How-to:
   Chop garlic, p. 27

Don't Panic: Chopping garlic may cause you concern, but the rest of it is just measuring, pouring, and layering.

1. Finely **chop** the garlic\* and **add** to a medium bowl along with the tomatoes, oregano, salt, red pepper, and black pepper (about 12 turns on a pepper mill). In a separate bowl, **mix** together the ricotta, 1 c. of the mozzarella, and the Parmesan. **Put** the spinach in a salad spinner, **wash,** and **spin** dry. Now you're ready to assemble.

2. In the bottom of a 5- to 6-qt. slow cooker, **spread** a thin layer of the sauce. **Top** with 4 of the noodles (breaking to fit as necessary.) **Spread** 1½ c. of the sauce over the noodles (be sure to **cover** completely with sauce so the noodles don't dry out). **Layer** with 2 c. of the spinach and 1½ c. of the cheese mixture Ⓐ. **Repeat** twice more with the noodles, sauce, spinach, and cheese mixture. **Top** with the remaining 4 noodles, sauce, and 1 c. mozzarella.

Ⓐ

3. **Cover** and **cook** on low until the noodles are tender, 3 to 3½ hours. **Test** the noodles for doneness by inserting a paring knife in the center of the lasagna (if it goes in easily, it's ready).

# Cacio e Pepe

The hardest part of this recipe is remembering to take the butter out of the fridge to let it soften. Otherwise, this is a "decadent but worth it" recipe I'd love you to learn how to make.

3 T. unsalted butter
1 to 2 tsp. whole black peppercorns
1 c. (4 oz.) grated pecorino
½ c. (2 oz.) grated Parmesan
1 box (1 lb.) whole wheat or regular spaghetti

Tools needed: large pot, colander, cutting board, small skillet, measuring cups and spoons, liquid measuring cup, cheese grater (if grating it yourself), silicone spatula, large bowl, kitchen timer.

**\* How-to:**
Crack black pepper, p. 38

Don't Panic: Cracking peppercorns with a pan is good exercise. Work it.

1. About an hour ahead of time, **take** the butter out of the refrigerator and let it come to room temperature.

2. **Fill** a large pot with water (to about 1 inch from the top). **Place** on the stove and **turn** the heat to high to bring to a boil. **Place** a colander in the sink. Meanwhile, **crack** the pepper using the bottom of a small skillet until all of the peppercorns are cracked.**\***

3. In a large bowl, using a silicone spatula, **combine** the pecorino, Parmesan, butter, and cracked pepper until the mixture is crumbly Ⓐ.

Ⓐ

4. When the water comes to a boil, **add** the pasta and **cook** according to the package directions. Once the pasta is al dente, **use** a liquid measuring cup to **take** ½ c. of the pasta water from the pot; **set aside.** **Drain** the pasta into the colander. Immediately **add** the pasta and ¼ c. of the pasta water to the large bowl and **stir** to combine until the cheeses have melted. **Add** more pasta water, if necessary, for a creamier consistency.

# SLAMMIN' PASTA WITH CLAMS

Afraid to make anything with clams? I promise you won't run screaming from your kitchen during the process.

2 dozen littleneck clams

3 cloves garlic

¼ c. chopped fresh flat-leaf parsley

1 c. dry white wine, such as sauvignon blanc

1 box (1 lb.) whole wheat or regular spaghetti

3 T. e.v. olive oil (2 T. + 1 T.)

¼ tsp. crushed red pepper, plus more to taste

Kosher salt, to taste

**Tools needed:** 2 large pots (1 lid), colander, large bowl, tongs, measuring cups and spoons, cutting board, chef's knife, kitchen timer, wooden spoon.

**\*** How-to:

Smash garlic, p. 26

Chop parsley, pp. 32–33

**Don't Panic:** Washing clams, smashing garlic, and chopping parsley—have at it!

1. **Fill** a large pot with water (to about 1 inch from the top). **Place** on the stove and **turn** the heat to high to bring to a boil. **Place** the clams in a colander. **Put** the colander in a large bowl in the sink and **fill** the bowl with cold water. Let the clams **soak** a few minutes, then **rub** with your fingers to dislodge any dirt; **drain. Throw** away any clams that remain open (they are dead).

2. **Smash** the garlic\* and **chop** the parsley.\* **Measure** the wine. **Place** your ingredients next to the stove.

3. When the water comes to a boil, **add** the pasta and **cook** according to the package directions. Meanwhile, **place** another large pot on the stove and **turn** the heat to medium. **Measure** and **pour** in 2 T. of the oil and **heat** until it shimmers (1 to 2 minutes). **Scoop** up the garlic with your chef's knife, **add** to the pot, and **cook**, stirring, for 30 seconds, until fragrant. **Add** the clams and wine (beware, it will splatter a bit) and **cover** the pot. **Wash** the colander and **return** it

Ⓐ

to the sink. **Cook** the clams until they open, about 8 minutes. **Discard** any that do not open. **Add** the parsley and ¼ tsp. red pepper Ⓐ.

4. Once the pasta is al dente, **drain** it into the colander and **transfer** to a large serving bowl. **Top** with the clams and **drizzle** with the remaining 1 T. oil. **Sprinkle** a tiny bit of salt and red pepper to taste.

# Pesto Pasta

Yes, there are a million pesto recipes out there—probably because it's so delicious and easy to make. This is a good time to master using a food processor. You can also use this as a veggie dip, or as a dressing for steamed vegetables, even a sandwich spread, you name it . . .

2 c. loosely packed basil
    leaves (about 1 bunch)
1 clove garlic
¼ c. pine nuts
¼ c. grated Parmesan, plus
    more for serving
1 tsp. kosher salt (¼ tsp. +
    ¾ tsp.)
⅛ tsp. freshly ground black
    pepper
⅓ c. e.v. olive oil
1 box (1 lb.) whole wheat
    or regular penne

Tools needed: food
processor, cheese grater
(if grating it yourself),
large pot, colander, liquid
measuring cup, measuring
cups and spoons, silicone
spatula, kitchen timer.

\* How-to:
    Smash and peel garlic,
      pp. 26–27
    Use a food processor,
      p. 16

Don't Panic: Using your food processor can be loud and off-putting. Don't shy away.

1. **Fill** a large pot with water (to about 1 inch from the top). **Place** on the stove and **turn** the heat to high to bring to a boil. **Place** a colander in the sink. **Pull** the basil leaves from the stems and **wash**. **Smash** and **peel** the garlic.\*

2. In a food processor,\* **combine** the basil, garlic, pine nuts, Parmesan, ¼ tsp. of the salt, and the pepper (about 6 turns on a pepper mill). **Press** On several times until finely chopped. **Scrape** down the sides with a silicone spatula. **Add** the oil and **pulse** a few times until the pesto is smooth and the oil is incorporated **A**.

**A**

3. When the water comes to a boil, **add** the pasta and **cook** according to the package directions. Once the pasta is al dente, **use** a liquid measuring cup to **take** ½ c. of the pasta water from the pot; **set aside**. **Drain** the pasta into the colander. **Return** the pasta to the pot along with the pesto and **toss** well. **Stir** in some of the reserved pasta water if the sauce is too thick. **Season** with the remaining ¾ tsp. salt. **Serve** topped with extra Parmesan, if you like.

# VEGETABLES

Broccoli with Golden Raisins & Garlic

Green Beans with Almonds

**Sautéed Spinach & Garlic**

SMASHED RED POTATOES WITH CHIVES

Roasted Asparagus with Lemon

ROASTED EGGPLANT & CHERRY TOMATOES

Roasted Cauliflower & Sage

**Roasted Brussels Sprouts**

OVEN FRIES

Roasted Lemon-Thyme Portobello Mushrooms

ROASTED SWEET POTATO COINS

MINTY SUGAR SNAPS

**Summer Tomato Bruschetta**

Mexican Corn · KALE CHIPS

# Broccoli with Golden Raisins & Garlic

This is an exciting way to serve broccoli—spicy, sweet, and savory.

1 bunch broccoli or 1 bag
   (1 lb.) frozen broccoli
   florets
3 cloves garlic
3 T. e.v. olive oil
¼ c. golden raisins
¼ tsp. crushed red pepper
½ tsp. kosher salt
¼ c. water

**Tools needed:** cutting board, chef's knife, strainer, large pot with lid, measuring cups and spoons, tongs, large spoon, kitchen timer.

**\*** How-to:
   Smash and peel garlic,
   pp. 26–27

**Buy** *broccoli with compact, bright green florets and sturdy (not bendable) stalks.* **Store** *unwashed in an unsealed plastic bag in the refrigerator for up to 5 days.*

**Don't Panic:** Cutting broccoli florets, smashing garlic, and not overcooking the brocs are the things to think about here—but all without worry.

1. **Cut** the fresh broccoli into florets, leaving about 2 inches of stem attached **Ⓐ**. I try to cut all the florets about the same size so they will cook in the same amount of time. **Place** them in a strainer and **pass** under cool running water to wash. **Smash** the garlic and **peel.\***

2. **Place** a large pot on the stove and **turn** the heat to medium. Measure and **pour** in the oil and **heat** until it shimmers (1 to 2 minutes). **Add** the garlic and **cook,** stirring, until light golden brown, about 2 minutes. Now that the oil is flavored, **use** tongs to **take** the garlic out and **discard Ⓑ**.

3. **Add** the fresh broccoli (or frozen broccoli, if using), raisins, red pepper, and salt to the pot and **stir** for about 30 seconds to coat with the oil. **Add** the water, **cover,** and let **steam** for 3 to 5 minutes. You want it to be tender but not mushy. **Stir** again and **serve.**

Ⓐ

Ⓑ

147

# Sautéed Spinach & Garlic

Does the word *sauté* scare you? It's easy—and cooking spinach this way is like a party in a pan.

2 large bunches spinach or
   1 bag (1 lb.) frozen leaf
   spinach
4 cloves garlic
2 T. e.v. olive oil
¼ tsp. kosher salt
¼ tsp. freshly ground black
   pepper

Tools needed: salad spinner, strainer (if needed), cutting board, chef's knife, large skillet, measuring spoons, tongs.

\* How-to:
   Smash and peel garlic,
   pp. 26–27

*Buy spinach with bright green leaves, not yellow or slimy. Store wrapped in paper towels in an unsealed plastic bag in the refrigerator for 3 to 4 days.*

Don't Panic: Smashing the garlic is easy, and don't let the large pile of spinach in the skillet scare you because it will shrink down as it cooks.

1. **Remove** and **discard** the tough stems from the fresh spinach (you should have about 16 c. of leaves). **Put** into a salad spinner, **wash,** and **spin** dry. (Or, if using frozen spinach, **put** in a strainer, and **pass** under warm water to thaw; **squeeze** out excess water.) **Smash** the garlic and **peel.**\*

2. **Place** a large skillet on the stove and **turn** the heat to medium. **Measure** and **pour** in the oil and **heat** until it shimmers (1 to 2 minutes). **Add** the garlic and **cook,** stirring, until fragrant (do not let it brown), about 1 minute. Now that the oil is flavored, **use** tongs to **take** the garlic out and **discard.**

3. **Add** half of the spinach (or all of the frozen spinach, if using) and **cook,** turning with tongs, until it begins to wilt, about 1 minute. I know this looks like a lot, but it will shrink down! **Add** the remaining spinach and **sprinkle** with the salt and pepper (about 12 turns on a pepper mill) and continue to **cook,** turning, until wilted, 2 to 3 minutes . **Serve.**

Ⓐ

# SMASHED RED POTATOES WITH CHIVES

These are not only easy (no knife skills required)—they're also exhilarating. You get to smash the potatoes when they're done. Using a nice, high-quality extra virgin olive oil makes a difference here.

1½ lbs. small red potatoes (about 8)
2 T. e.v. olive oil
1 small hunk of Parmesan
8 fresh chives
¼ tsp. kosher or sea salt
⅛ tsp. freshly ground black pepper

**Tools needed:** medium saucepan, kitchen timer, paring knife, colander, tongs, cutting board, metal spatula, measuring spoons, vegetable peeler, scissors.

*Buy potatoes that are firm, without cracks or sprouts. Store in a cool dark place like your pantry for up to 2 weeks.*

Don't Panic: Nothing to worry about here, sweeties.

1. **Wash** your potatoes (no need to peel them). **Place** them in a medium saucepan, **cover** with cold water by 2 inches, and **place** on the stove. **Turn** the heat to high and **let** come to a boil. Then **lower** the heat to medium and **simmer** (low boil) until the potatoes are very tender and easily pierced with the tip of a paring knife, 15 to 18 minutes. **Drain** into a colander in the sink.

2. Use tongs to **place** a hot potato on a cutting board. **Rest** a small plate on top of it and gently **smash** it semiflat **Ⓐ**. Use a metal spatula to **scoop** up the potato and **slide** onto a serving plate **Ⓑ**. **Do** the same with the rest of the potatoes.

3. **Drizzle** the potatoes with the oil. Using a vegetable peeler, **shave** small pieces of the Parmesan (about ¼ c. or as much as you want) over the potatoes. Use scissors to **snip** the chives into small pieces right over the potatoes. **Sprinkle** with the salt and pepper (about 6 turns on a pepper mill).

Ⓐ

Ⓑ

# Roasted Asparagus with Lemon

This recipe will make you look like you really know what you're doing.

1 pound asparagus
1 T. e.v. olive oil
Grated zest of 1 lemon
  (about 1 tsp.)
¼ tsp. kosher salt
¼ tsp. freshly ground black
  pepper

Tools needed: rimmed
sheet pan, measuring
spoons, grater/zester,
kitchen timer.

**\*** How-to:
  Zest citrus, p. 24

*Buy asparagus that is perky, and not at all limp (it's usually sold in 1-pound bundles). **Store** unwashed in an unsealed plastic bag in the refrigerator for 3 to 4 days.*

Don't Panic: The only challenge here is grating the lemon zest.

1. **Heat** the oven (with the oven rack in the middle) to 425°F. **Wash** the asparagus and **snap** off and **discard** the tough bottom end (about 2 inches) from each spear **A**.

**A**

2. **Place** the asparagus in the center of a rimmed sheet pan and **drizzle** with the oil. **Wash** and **dry** the outside of the lemon and **grate** the zest directly onto the asparagus. **Sprinkle** with the salt and pepper (about 12 turns on a pepper mill). **Toss** together with your hands and then **spread** into a single layer (see p. 144). **Roast** until just tender, about 10 minutes.

# ROASTED EGGPLANT & CHERRY TOMATOES

Cooking eggplant seems difficult and labor intensive, doesn't it? Well, here it's not. You can also spread this on a slice of crusty country bread or use as a pasta sauce. Or fab leftovers.

1 large eggplant (about
   1½ lbs.)
4 cloves garlic
1 pint cherry or grape
   tomatoes
6 sprigs thyme
⅓ c. e.v. olive oil
¾ tsp. kosher salt
¼ tsp. crushed red pepper
¼ tsp. freshly ground black
   pepper

Tools needed: 2½- to 3-qt. baking dish, cutting board, chef's knife, measuring cups and spoons, large spoon, kitchen timer.

**\*** How-to:
   Smash and peel garlic,
   pp. 26–27

*Buy eggplant that is smooth-skinned, evenly firm, and without soft spots. Store in the refrigerator for 3 to 4 days.*

Don't Panic: Cutting the eggplant into cubes is a cinch, I promise.

1. **Heat** the oven (with the oven rack in the middle) to 400°F. **Wash** the eggplant (no need to peel). **Cut off** and **discard** the stem. Next, **cut** the eggplant into 1-inch-thick rounds. **Stack** 2 rounds at a time, then **cut** into 1-inch cubes **Ⓐ**. **Smash** the garlic and **peel.\***

2. **Place** the eggplant and garlic in a 2½- to 3-qt. baking dish. **Wash** the tomatoes and thyme and **add** to the dish. **Drizzle** with the oil and **sprinkle** with the salt, red pepper, and black pepper (about 12 turns on a pepper mill) **Ⓑ**. **Toss** together with your hands until the eggplant is coated with oil (a little overcrowding in the dish is okay).

3. **Roast** until the eggplant is really soft and tender, 50 to 60 minutes. (Set your timer, and at 40 minutes, give the vegetables a quick stir.)

Ⓐ          Ⓑ

# Roasted Cauliflower & Sage

First of all, cauliflower is very good for the bod, plus, the delicious, sweet flavor makes this recipe vital to your repertoire.

1 medium head cauliflower
12 fresh sage leaves
2 T. e.v. olive oil
¼ tsp. kosher salt
¼ tsp. freshly ground
   black pepper

**Tools needed:** cutting board, chef's knife, colander, rimmed sheet pan, measuring spoons, kitchen timer, pot holders, metal spatula, paring knife.

*Buy cauliflower that is uniformly white and without dark spots. Store unwashed in an unsealed plastic bag in the refrigerator for up to 5 days.*

Don't Panic: Cutting a cauliflower into small, bite-size florets can be daunting. Let's do it together.

1. **Heat** the oven (with the oven rack in the middle) to 425°F. **Snap** off and **discard** the green leaves from the bottom of the cauliflower. **Break** off large florets from the stem  or, if it's easier, you can use your chef's knife to **cut** them away from the stem. Then **cut** them into bite-size florets; **discard** the stem. Try to cut each floret about the same size so everything cooks evenly—this is the hardest part. Hang in there! **Place** the florets in a colander and **pass** under cool running water to wash. **Transfer** to a rimmed sheet pan.

   Ⓐ

2. **Push** the cauliflower toward the center of the pan. **Pick** the sage leaves from their stems and **add** to the pan. **Drizzle** with the oil and **sprinkle** with the salt and pepper (about 12 turns on a pepper mill). **Toss** together with your hands and **spread** into a single layer.

3. **Roast** for 15 minutes, then **pull** the pan out of the oven and **turn** the cauliflower with a spatula. **Return** to the oven to finish cooking until golden brown and tender, 10 to 15 minutes more. You'll know the florets are done when they are golden brown and can be easily pierced with the tip of a paring knife.

# Roasted Brussels Sprouts

Are you a brussels sprout hater? Lots of people are! If I convince you to try these, I bet you'll change your mind. For the lovers, take it to the next level by squeezing some fresh lemon juice over the roasted brussels sprouts and sprinkling with some grated Parmesan.

1 lb. brussels sprouts
   (about 22 medium)
1 clove garlic
2 T. e.v. olive oil
½ tsp. kosher salt
¼ tsp. freshly ground
   black pepper

Tools needed: strainer, cutting board, paring knife, measuring spoons, rimmed sheet pan, kitchen timer.

**\*** How-to:
   Chop garlic, p. 27

***Buy** brussels sprouts with bright green, tightly packed leaves. **Store** unwashed in an unsealed plastic bag in the refrigerator for 3 to 4 days.*

Don't Panic: Trimming brussels sprouts and chopping garlic is not a calamity. I know you thrive on adversity anyway.

1. **Heat** the oven (with the oven rack in the middle) to 425°F. **Place** the brussels sprouts in a strainer and **pass** under cool running water to wash. With a paring knife, **trim** the ends off of each and **discard** any discolored leaves Ⓐ. **Cut** the sprouts in half lengthwise and **transfer** to a rimmed sheet pan. **Chop** the garlic.**\***

2. **Push** the sprouts toward the center of the pan, **drizzle** with the oil, and **sprinkle** with the garlic, salt, and pepper (about 12 turns on a pepper mill). **Toss** together with your hands. **Turn** the sprouts cut side down on the pan Ⓑ and **roast** 20 to 25 minutes. You know they are done when you **flip** them over and they are browned and can be easily pierced with the tip of a paring knife.

Ⓐ

Ⓑ

161

# Roasted Lemon-Thyme Portobello Mushrooms

I'm a former hater of the portobello. These changed me forever.

4 large portobello
   mushrooms
2 T. unsalted butter
1 T. fresh lemon juice
½ tsp. kosher salt
¼ tsp. freshly ground
   black pepper
1 T. fresh thyme leaves
   (about 4 sprigs)

Tools needed: roasting
pan, small skillet, measuring spoons, pastry brush,
kitchen timer, paring knife,
cutting board, chef's knife.

*How-to:
   Juice citrus, p. 25

*Buy mushrooms
that are firm, dry
(not slippery), and
without blemishes.
Store unwashed in
a paper bag in the
refrigerator for up to
5 days.*

Don't Panic: Wiping off the dirt on the mushrooms and making the
butter sauce are hardly problems for you.

1. **Heat** the oven (with the oven rack in the middle) to 425°F. **Break** off
   and **discard** the stems at the base of the mushroom. Using a damp
   paper towel, **wipe** off any visible dirt Ⓐ. **Place** the caps, tops up, in
   a roasting pan large enough to hold them in a single layer. **Juice** the
   lemon.*

2. **Place** a small skillet on the stove and **add** the butter, lemon juice,
   salt, and pepper (about 12 turns on a pepper mill). **Pull** the thyme
   leaves from their stems and **add**. **Turn** the heat to medium and **melt**
   the butter, then **remove** the pan from the heat.

3. Using a pastry brush or a spoon, **brush** some of the melted butter
   over the mushroom caps just to coat Ⓑ. **Flip** them over and **brush**
   the undersides with the remaining butter. **Transfer** to the oven and
   **roast** until the mushrooms are tender and the centers are easily
   pierced with the tip of a paring knife, 25 to 30 minutes. **Move** to a
   cutting board, **slice,** and **serve.** (If you like, make double the amount
   of lemon butter and use the extra for serving.)

Ⓐ

Ⓑ

# ROASTED SWEET POTATO COINS

Okay, you can nail this. The flavor is beyond. This is a great first step forward for a Can't Cook. Wherever you are in the world, whether you call them yams or sweet potatoes, I'm referring to the root vegetable with the bright orange flesh.

2 T. dark brown sugar
½ tsp. kosher salt
¼ tsp. ground cumin
¼ tsp. freshly ground black pepper
3 medium sweet potatoes (about 1½ lbs.)
2 T. e.v. olive oil

Tools needed: cutting board, chef's knife, rimmed sheet pan, small bowl, measuring spoons, kitchen timer, paring knife.

*Buy the ones often labeled garnet yams, with dark brown skin and bright orange flesh. Store in a cool dark place like your pantry for up to 2 weeks.*

Don't Panic: Slicing the potatoes into rounds (or coins) is all you!

1. **Heat** the oven (with the oven rack in the middle) to 425°F. In a small bowl, **combine** the brown sugar, salt, cumin, and pepper (about 12 turns on a pepper mill).

2. **Wash** the sweet potatoes (no need to peel). Make sure you have a firm grip on the potato, keeping your fingers out of the way, then **cut** it crosswise into ½-inch-thick rounds **Ⓐ**. **Transfer** to a rimmed sheet pan. **Drizzle** with the oil and **sprinkle** with the brown sugar mixture. Using your hands, **toss** to coat **Ⓑ**. **Spread** into a single layer without overlapping. **Roast** until the potatoes are tender and can be easily pierced with the tip of a paring knife, 25 to 30 minutes.

Ⓐ

Ⓑ

# MINTY SUGAR SNAPS

I beg you to try these. I make these often because they're such a crowd-pleaser. Delicious served cold, too.

1 pound sugar snap peas
2 shallots
15 fresh mint leaves
1 T. unsalted butter
¼ tsp. kosher salt
¼ tsp. freshly ground black pepper

**Tools needed:** strainer, cutting board, chef's knife, medium skillet, measuring spoons, wooden spoon.

**\*How-to:**
Slice shallots, p. 30

*Buy sugar snap peas that are bright green and without brown spots. Store unwashed in an unsealed plastic bag in the refrigerator for 3 to 4 days.*

**Don't Panic:** Slicing a shallot is in the "How-to" section, so you can definitely make this happen.

1. Using your fingers, **snap** the stems off the snap peas. Often, a string is attached to the stem. **Pull** and **discard** both Ⓐ. **Place** the snap peas in a strainer and **pass** under cool running water to wash. Using a chef's knife, **trim** off each end of each shallot and **peel. Slice** into thin rings.**\* Wash** and **dry** the mint leaves.

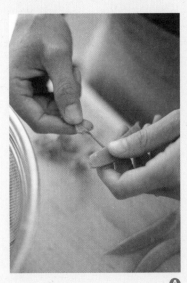 

Ⓐ        Ⓑ

2. **Place** your medium skillet on the stove and **turn** the heat to medium. **Add** the butter. Once it's melted, **add** the shallots and **cook**, stirring with a wooden spoon, for 1 minute, until softened. **Add** the snap peas and **cook**, stirring often, until crisp-tender, 3 to 4 minutes Ⓑ. **Stir** in the mint, salt, and pepper (about 12 turns on a pepper mill). **Serve** immediately.

# Summer Tomato Bruschetta

Nothing screams "QUICK! EASY MEAL!" when I'm short on time as much as bruschetta does. Grape or cherry tomatoes make this a cinch. Of course, you can use beautiful whole summer tomatoes if you can handle dicing them.

2 pints grape or cherry
   tomatoes
2 cloves garlic
10 fresh basil leaves
½ tsp. kosher salt
¼ tsp. freshly ground black
   pepper
2 tsp. balsamic vinegar
¼ cup e.v. olive oil (2 T. + 2 T.)
½ of a baguette

Tools needed: cutting
board, chef's knife,
serrated knife, medium
bowl, rimmed sheet pan,
measuring spoons, pastry
brush.

\* How-to:
   Chop garlic, p. 27

**Buy** *tomatoes that
are plump and bright
red and actually
smell like tomatoes.*
**Store** *unwashed at
room temperature
(not in the fridge!)
for up to 5 days.*

Don't Panic: Slicing a baguette through the middle is not so easy. Keep your fingers out of the way by using a flat hand on top.

1. **Wash** the tomatoes. **Cut** them into quarters and **put** in a medium bowl. **Chop** the garlic.\* **Wash** and **tear** the basil. **Add** to the bowl along with the salt and pepper (about 12 turns on a pepper mill). **Drizzle** in the balsamic and 2 T. of the oil and **toss** well.

2. **Heat** the broiler (with the oven rack about 4 inches from the top). You're using only half of a baguette here. Using a serrated knife, **slice** it in half horizontally **Ⓐ**. **Place** the halves on a rimmed sheet pan cut side up and **brush** with the remaining 2 T. oil. **Broil** until golden brown and toasted, 1 to 2 minutes.

3. **Spoon** the tomato mixture over the toasted bread, then **cut** into smaller pieces for easy holding **Ⓑ**.

Ⓐ

Ⓑ

# Mexican Corn

Once you've mastered boiling corn, how about one additional easy step?
Go on . . .

4 ears fresh summer corn
½ c. grated Parmesan
⅛ to ¼ tsp. cayenne
   pepper
2 T. unsalted butter
2 limes

**Tools needed:** large pot,
colander, kitchen timer,
tongs, measuring cups and
spoons, cutting board,
cheese grater (if grating it
yourself), paring knife.

*Buy corn with
a bright green,
tight-fitting (not
dried-out) husk.
Peel back the husk
to make sure the
kernels are plump
and run all the way
to the tip. Store in
the refrigerator for
up to 2 days.*

Don't Panic: Flossing your teeth after you've eaten is more difficult
than making this recipe.

1. **Fill** a large pot with water to about 3 inches from the top and
   **place** on the stove. **Turn** the heat to high to **bring** to a boil. **Place**
   a colander in the sink. **Remove** the husks and silk from the corn.
   **Lower** the corn into the pot of boiling water. Once the water returns
   to a boil, **cook** the corn 5 minutes more. **Drain** the corn into the
   colander.

2. On a plate, **combine** the Parmesan and cayenne. **Rub** ½ T. of the
   butter over each ear of corn Ⓐ, then roll in the Parmesan mixture
   Ⓑ. **Cut** the limes into wedges and **serve** alongside the corn for
   squeezing.

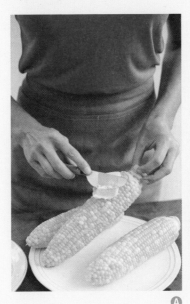

Ⓐ

Ⓑ

# KALE CHIPS

While you can certainly buy these in the store, it's super easy to make them fresh in your own kitchen. They are so light and crispy, even a non–kale eater will love these. Spice them with other seasonings like grated Parmesan, lemon pepper, curry or garlic powder, toasted sesame seeds, or a little cayenne pepper.

1 large bunch kale
3 T. e.v. olive oil
Kosher salt or sea salt
  flakes, to taste

Tools needed: rimmed sheet pan, salad spinner, measuring spoons, kitchen timer.

* How-to:
  Season to taste, p. 39

*Buy kale that has perky dark green leaves, without any yellow. Store unwashed in an unsealed plastic bag in the refrigerator for 4 to 5 days.*

Don't Panic: Making sure each leaf is fully coated with just enough oil is important for the right crispness.

1. **Heat** the oven (with the oven rack in the middle) to 300°F. **Pull** the kale leaves from the stem; **discard** the stem. **Tear** the leaves into 3-inch pieces (about 10 c. total) and **put** into a salad spinner. **Wash, spin** dry, and **place** on a rimmed sheet pan.

2. **Drizzle** the leaves with the oil and **toss. Rub** each leaf so it is evenly coated with oil Ⓐ. **Arrange** in a single layer and **bake** until crisp, 20 to 25 minutes. **Let cool,** then **sprinkle** on a tiny bit of salt to taste* before serving.

Ⓐ

175

# GRAINS & BEANS

## Brown Rice Pilaf
## SWEET PEA BULGUR WHEAT PILAF
## Toasted Pine Nut & Cranberry Quinoa
## Couscous Salad with Chickpeas, Tomatoes & Mint
## Garlic & Rosemary Cannellini Beans
## Stir-fried Rice with Sunny-side Up Eggs

# Brown Rice Pilaf

This is a stunningly easy recipe that you will serve dozens and dozens of times from here on out. It's a wildly popular standby side dish at our house.

1 clove garlic
1 c. brown rice or brown rice blend
2 c. water
1 T. e.v. olive oil
2 bay leaves
½ tsp. kosher salt

Tools needed: medium saucepan with lid, cutting board, chef's knife, measuring cups and spoons, wooden spoon, kitchen timer.

*How-to:
Smash and peel garlic, pp. 26–27

Don't Panic: Smashing the garlic and waiting for that moment when the rice is tender and the water is absorbed are nothing for someone with your level of brilliance.

1. Let's get started. First, **smash** and **peel** the garlic* and **measure** the rice and water.

2. **Place** a medium saucepan on the stove and **turn** the heat to medium-high. **Measure** and **pour** in the oil and **heat** until it shimmers (1 to 2 minutes). **Add** the garlic and **cook,** stirring with a wooden spoon, until fragrant (do not let brown), about 1 minute.

3. **Add** the rice and **stir** a few times to coat in the oil Ⓐ. **Add** the water, bay leaves, and salt and let come to a boil. **Cover** the pan, **lower** the heat to low, and **simmer** (low boil) until the rice is tender and the water is absorbed, 45 to 50 minutes. **Discard** the bay leaves before serving.

Ⓐ

# SWEET PEA BULGUR WHEAT PILAF

Bulgur is a "superfood" (translation: we are supposed to be eating lots of it because it's good for us). As an added bonus, it cooks quickly and easily and is completely delicious. Nice, right?

1 small yellow onion
2 T. e.v. olive oil
½ tsp. kosher salt
1 c. bulgur wheat
1¾ c. water
1½ c. frozen peas
⅛ tsp. freshly ground black
   pepper

Tools needed: cutting
board, chef's knife,
measuring cups and
spoons, medium saucepan
with lid, wooden spoon,
strainer, kitchen timer.

*How-to:
   Chop an onion, p. 29

Don't Panic: Chopping an onion may make you feel worried, and even want to cry, but it's essential to becoming a FORMER Can't Cook.

1. First off, **chop** the onion.*

2. **Place** a medium saucepan on the stove and **turn** the heat to medium-high. **Measure** and **pour** in the oil and **heat** until it shimmers (1 to 2 minutes). **Add** the onion and salt and **cook**, stirring often with a wooden spoon, until softened, 3 to 5 minutes. While the onion cooks, **measure** the bulgur and the water and **put** near the stove.

3. **Add** the bulgur and **stir** so it is coated with the oil. **Pour** in the water and let come to a boil. **Cover, lower** the heat to low, and **cook** 10 minutes. Meanwhile, **place** the frozen peas in a strainer and **pass** under hot running water until thawed.

4. After 10 minutes, quickly **stir** in the peas, **cover** again, and **turn off** the heat. **Let sit** for 5 minutes more. **Season** with the pepper (about 6 turns on a pepper mill) and **serve.**

# Toasted Pine Nut & Cranberry Quinoa

It may be hard to pronounce, but that doesn't mean it's hard to make! That's the dirty secret about quinoa (keen-wa). Here we have a nice vegetarian meal (or side dish), made in 25 minutes.

¼ c. pine nuts or sliced almonds

½ c. dried cranberries, cherries, or raisins

1 c. quinoa

1½ c. water

¼ tsp. ground cinnamon

¼ tsp. ground or grated whole nutmeg (about 12 passes on a grater)

¾ tsp. kosher salt

¼ tsp. freshly ground black pepper

1 T. e.v. olive oil

**Tools needed:** medium saucepan with lid, measuring cups and spoons, cutting board, chef's knife, grater/zester, kitchen timer.

Don't Panic: A watched pine nut never burns . . .

1. **Measure** the pine nuts (or almonds), cranberries (or other fruit), quinoa, and water and **place** them near the stove along with the cinnamon, nutmeg, salt, and pepper.

2. **Place** a medium saucepan on the stove and **turn** the heat to medium. **Measure** and **pour** in the oil and **heat** until it shimmers (1 to 2 minutes). **Add** the pine nuts (or almonds) and **cook**, stirring with a wooden spoon, until toasted and fragrant, 2 to 3 minutes.

3. **Stir** in the cranberries Ⓐ (or other fruit), quinoa, cinnamon, nutmeg, salt, and pepper (about 12 turns on a pepper mill). **Add** the water and let come to a boil. **Cover, lower** the heat to low, and **simmer** (low boil) until the water is absorbed and the quinoa is tender and fluffy, 15 to 18 minutes.

Ⓐ

183

# Couscous Salad with Chickpeas, Tomatoes & Mint

I thought you might appreciate not having to turn on the stove. A delicious year-round side dish or light lunch.

1 c. whole wheat or plain couscous

1¼ c. very hot tap water

4 scallions

1 c. grape tomatoes

1 can (15 oz.) chickpeas

3 T. fresh lemon juice (about 1 lemon)

15 fresh mint leaves

2 T. e.v. olive oil

½ tsp. kosher salt

¼ tsp. freshly ground black pepper

Tools needed: large bowl, measuring cups and spoons, liquid measuring cup, cutting board, chef's knife, strainer, citrus juicer, fork, kitchen timer.

**\*** How-to:
Slice scallions, p. 31
Juice citrus, p. 25

Don't Panic: All you need to do is chop and toss. Okay, a little squeezing, too . . . but it's all within your ability.

1. In a large bowl, **combine** the couscous and hot water, **cover** tightly with plastic wrap or a large plate, and **let stand** until the water is absorbed and the couscous is tender, about 10 minutes.

2. Meanwhile, **cut off** the roots from the scallions and **peel off** and **discard** the outer membrane. **Wash** and then thinly **slice** the white and light green parts into rounds.**\*** **Wash** the tomatoes and **cut** in half, **drain** and **rinse** the chickpeas, and **juice** the lemon.**\***

3. When the couscous is tender, **fluff** it with a fork **Ⓐ** and **add** in your prepped ingredients. **Tear** the mint leaves in half **Ⓑ** and **add** to the bowl along with the oil, salt, and pepper (about 12 turns on a pepper mill). **Stir** to combine.

Ⓐ

Ⓑ

# Garlic & Rosemary Cannellini Beans

A one-pot dish that serves as a vegetarian meal or fab side dish. You can serve this as is, over pasta, or with a big delicious slab of toasted country bread.

2 medium carrots
2 cloves garlic
2 tsp. chopped fresh
   rosemary (about 1 sprig)
1 can (15 oz.) diced
   tomatoes
2 cans (15 oz. each)
   cannellini beans
1 T. e.v. olive oil
⅓ c. water
¼ tsp. kosher salt
¼ tsp. freshly ground
   black pepper
2 T. grated Parmesan

Tools needed: vegetable peeler, cutting board, chef's knife, measuring cups and spoons, can opener, strainer, medium saucepan, wooden spoon, kitchen timer, cheese grater (if grating it yourself).

*How-to:
   Chop garlic, p. 27
   Chop rosemary,
      pp. 32–33

Don't Panic: Chopping the garlic and cutting carrots? You own this.

1. **Peel** the carrots and **cut** them in half lengthwise, then thinly **slice** them crosswise into half-moons. **Chop** the garlic* and the rosemary.* **Open** the can of tomatoes and **drain** and **rinse** the beans. **Set up** your ingredients next to the stove **Ⓐ**.

2. **Place** a medium saucepan on the stove and **turn** the heat to medium. **Measure** and **pour** in the oil and **heat** until it shimmers (1 to 2 minutes). **Scoop** up the chopped garlic with your knife and **add** to the pan. **Cook**, stirring with a wooden spoon, until fragrant, about 30 seconds.

**Ⓐ**

3. **Add** the carrots, tomatoes, beans, water, rosemary, salt, and pepper (about 12 turns on a pepper mill). Let come to a boil, then **lower** the heat to medium-low and **simmer** (low boil), stirring occasionally, until the carrots are tender, 15 to 20 minutes. **Stir** in the Parmesan and **serve**.

# Stir-fried Rice with Sunny-side Up Eggs

I am not winning any nutrition prizes for this one, because I cook the finished rice in bacon fat. However, the flavor is breathtaking and it's a nice way to use up leftover rice. Just eat it in moderation—for breakfast, lunch, or dinner. And HEY! No knives used in this recipe.

5 oz. fresh baby spinach (about 6 packed c.)

4 strips bacon

3 c. cold "leftover" brown rice (already cooked)

2 T. low-sodium soy sauce

4 large eggs

Freshly ground black pepper, to taste

**Tools needed:** salad spinner, large skillet with lid, measuring cups and spoons, wooden spoon, tongs.

To make 3 c. cooked brown rice, put 1 c. brown rice and 2 c. water in a medium saucepan. Bring to a boil, cover, lower the heat to low, and simmer until the rice is tender and the water is absorbed, 45 to 50 minutes. Transfer to a storage container and refrigerate until cold.

**Don't Panic:** Cooking spinach can frighten people, but it's definitely in your range. P.S.—You can use 1 c. frozen peas instead.

1. **Put** the spinach into a salad spinner, **wash,** and **spin** dry.

2. **Place** a large skillet on the stove and **turn** the heat to medium. **Add** the bacon and **cook,** turning once or twice with tongs, until crisp, 6 to 8 minutes. **Transfer** the bacon to a paper towel–lined plate, leaving the drippings in the skillet (you should have about 2 T.). Or, if you prefer, you can pour off the drippings . . . but leave the flavorful browned bits in the bottom of the skillet.

3. **Stir** in the cooked rice and soy sauce with a wooden spoon, scraping up the browned bits, and **cook** over medium heat, stirring, until heated through, 1 to 2 minutes. **Put** the spinach on top of the rice and **cover** the skillet. Let the spinach **steam** for 1 to 2 minutes until it wilts. Then, using your tongs, **fold** the spinach into the rice.

4. **Lower** the heat to medium-low and, using your tongs, **make** 4 small wells in the rice. Carefully **crack** the eggs directly into each well. **Cover** and **cook** until the whites are just set and the yolks are soft to the touch, 3 to 5 minutes. **Break** the bacon over the rice and eggs, and if you are comfortable, **season** with pepper to taste. **Serve** immediately.

# Salads

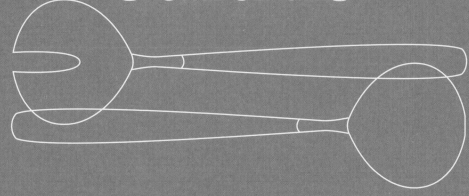

**Kale Salads–3 Easy Recipes!**

**Butter Lettuce Salad with Pine Nuts & Parsley**

Warm Spinach Salad
with Blue Cheese

TOMATO & WATERMELON SALAD WITH TOASTED ALMONDS

**Chicken Salad with Apples & Basil**

# Butter Lettuce Salad with Pine Nuts & Parsley

This can be your go-to green salad. It appears fancy-pants but the steps couldn't be simpler. This makes a large batch of vinaigrette, so you can have dressing all week.

¼ c. pine nuts
1 head butter lettuce
¼ c. fresh flat-leaf parsley
    leaves

**For the vinaigrette
(large batch):**
1 T. Dijon mustard
¼ c. red wine vinegar
½ c. e.v. olive oil
¾ tsp. kosher salt
½ tsp. freshly ground black
    pepper

**Tools needed:** small
skillet, salad spinner,
large salad bowl, small
bowl, measuring cups and
spoons, whisk, tongs.

**\* How-to:**
    Toast pine nuts, p. 37

Don't Panic: Toasting pine nuts might be new for you, but No Prior Job Experience is necessary.

1. **Place** a small skillet on the stove and **add** the pine nuts. **Turn** the heat to medium. **Stir** or **shake** the nuts often (so they cook evenly) until lightly toasted and fragrant, 3 to 4 minutes.**\*** **Remove** from the heat.

2. **Discard** any discolored outer leaves from the head of lettuce. **Tear** the lettuce into bite-size pieces (about 8 c.) and **put** into a salad spinner. **Wash, spin** dry, and **place** in a large salad bowl. **Wash** the parsley, then **pick** the leaves from the stems (a hearty handful) and **add** to the bowl.

3. For the vinaigrette: In a small bowl, **measure** and **whisk** together the mustard, vinegar, oil, salt, and pepper (about 24 turns on a pepper mill).

4. **Drizzle** about 4 T. of the vinaigrette (or however much you like) over the lettuce and **add** the toasted pine nuts. **Use** tongs to **toss** well. **Serve** immediately.

5. **Store** the remaining vinaigrette in a jar in the fridge for up to 2 weeks. Just **shake** it up before using.

    Take it to the next level with these mix-ins:
    Crumbled goat or blue cheese
    Orange or grapefruit sections and avocado slices
    More herbs, like tarragon and chives
    Halved cherry tomatoes and sliced cucumbers

# Warm Spinach Salad with Blue Cheese

This is a nice lunch salad or side dish. What sets it apart is the warm vinaigrette poured over the spinach. The onions give it a little crunch and the blue cheese a savory tang.

1 large bunch fresh spinach
1 small red onion
2 T. e.v. olive oil
2 T. honey
2 T. red wine vinegar
2 T. Dijon mustard
¼ tsp. kosher salt
¼ tsp. freshly ground black
　　pepper
4 oz. blue cheese
　　(1 c. crumbled)

Tools needed: salad spinner, large salad bowl, cutting board, chef's knife, medium skillet, measuring cups and spoons, whisk, tongs.

*How-to:
　Slice an onion, p. 29

Don't Panic: Making your own vinaigrette requires just measuring and pouring, and you may raise an eyebrow at slicing the onions. Impress yourself today by diving in.

1. **Tear off** and **discard** the tough stems from the spinach. **Put** the leaves in a salad spinner, **wash, spin** dry (you should have 8 to 10 c.), and **place** in a large salad bowl.

2. **Slice** the onion into thin half-moons and **set aside.***

3. For the vinaigrette: **Place** a medium skillet on the stove. **Add** the oil, honey, vinegar, mustard, salt, and pepper (about 12 turns on a pepper mill) and **whisk** together. **Turn** the heat to medium. **Add** the sliced onion and **cook**, turning with tongs, until the onion is softened but still a little crunchy, 2 to 3 minutes.

4. **Pour** the warm vinaigrette and onion over the salad and **toss** well with tongs. **Crumble** the blue cheese over the top and **serve** immediately.

# Tomato & Watermelon Salad with Toasted Almonds

The perfect summer salad: crunchy, savory, and sweet . . .

½ c. sliced almonds

2 large beefsteak tomatoes (about 1 lb. total)

1 Kirby cucumber (or ½ of a regular cucumber, peeled)

½ small seedless watermelon

2 T. e.v. olive oil

1 T. sherry vinegar or red wine vinegar

¼ tsp. kosher salt or sea salt flakes

¼ tsp. freshly ground black pepper

**Tools needed:** cutting board, chef's knife, small skillet, measuring cups and spoons, large platter or plate.

**\*** How-to:

Toast sliced almonds, p. 37

**Don't Panic:** Toasting the almonds is a new thing for you, I'll bet. Adding a nice crunch of protein is a step worth taking in your life. Also, if you buy half a melon, you won't have to cut into a whole one (yikes!).

1. **Place** a small skillet on the stove and **add** the almonds. **Turn** the heat to medium. **Stir** or **shake** the almonds often (so they cook evenly) until toasted and fragrant, 3 to 5 minutes.**\* Remove** from the heat. **Wash** the tomatoes and cucumber (you don't have to peel the Kirby).

2. Using your chef's knife, **cut** the tomatoes into wedges, then **cut off** the core. **Arrange** on a platter or plate as haphazardly as you wish. **Halve** the cucumber lengthwise, then **cut** it crosswise into half-moons and **add**. Using a round 1 tsp.-size measuring spoon, **scoop** out 2 cups of pieces from the watermelon half Ⓐ and **add** to the platter. **Sprinkle** the toasted almonds over the top. **Drizzle** with the oil and vinegar and **season** with the salt and pepper.

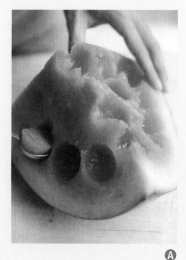

Ⓐ

# Chicken Salad with Apples & Basil

I love this salad for you. You will easily learn how to poach chicken for the rest of your life, and make a gorgeous, healthy meal at the same time.

3 boneless, skinless chicken breasts (6 to 8 oz. each)
¼ c. fresh lemon juice (about 2 lemons)
2 scallions
1 Granny Smith apple
2 T. e.v. olive oil
¾ tsp. kosher salt
¼ tsp. freshly ground black pepper
15 fresh basil leaves
¼ c. shelled roasted pistachios
¼ c. golden raisins

**Tools needed:** medium saucepan with lid, cutting board, chef's knife, large bowl, measuring cups and spoons, melon baller (optional), citrus juicer, tongs.

**\* How-to:**
Juice citrus, p. 25
Slice scallions, p. 31

**Don't Panic:** Poaching chicken sounds frightening, but don't shy away—you will love yourself for learning how.

1. **Wash** the chicken and **place** in a medium saucepan, then **cover** with cold water by 1 inch. **Place** on the stove and **turn** the heat to high. **Bring** to a boil. **Cover** and **remove** from the heat. **Let stand** for 15 minutes to cook through. Using tongs, **transfer** the chicken to a plate to cool. (The chicken can be poached up to 1 day in advance and refrigerated.) **Discard** the water.

2. Meanwhile, **take** out a large bowl. **Juice** the lemons,* **measure** ¼ c., and **pour** into the bowl. **Cut off** the roots from the scallions and **peel off** and **discard** the outer membrane. **Wash** and then thinly **slice** the white and light green part into rounds;* **add** to the bowl.

3. **Cut** the apple in half and **remove** the core with a round 1 tsp.-size measuring spoon or melon baller, if you have one. **Cut** each half into quarters, then **slice** crosswise into small pieces. **Add** to the bowl along with the oil, salt, and pepper (about 12 turns on a pepper mill). **Toss. Cut** the cooled chicken into bite-size pieces and **add** to the bowl. **Tear** the basil and **stir** in along with the pistachios and raisins.

# DESSERTS

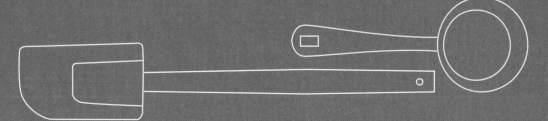

Chocolate Chip Cookies

**Oatmeal, Maple & Raisin Cookies**

**Chocolate Chia Drops**

PEANUT BUTTER DROPS

**Cherry-Ginger-Almond Drops**

Flourless Fudge Cake with Whipped Cream

BROILED HONEY-NUT BANANAS

Marinated Strawberries with Ice Cream

**Mixed Berry Crisp**

# Chocolate Chip Cookies

Julian Seinfeld loves to bake these cookies. He is a child. I know you can make them, too.

12 T. (1½ sticks) unsalted
   butter
1¼ c. all-purpose flour
1 c. whole wheat flour
½ tsp. baking soda
½ tsp. baking powder
¾ tsp. kosher salt
1 c. packed dark brown
   sugar
½ c. granulated sugar
1 large egg
1 tsp. pure vanilla extract
12 oz. semisweet
   chocolate chips

Tools needed: 2 rimmed
sheet pans, parchment
paper, medium bowl, large
mixing bowl, electric mixer
or wooden spoon, silicone
spatula, measuring cups
and spoons, large spoon,
wire rack, kitchen timer,
metal spatula.

*How-to:
   Measure flour, p. 42

**Don't Panic:** Remembering to take the butter out way beforehand always trips me up. Other than that, it's measuring and mixing. At the end, you get a cookie prize.

1. At least an hour beforehand, **take** the butter out of the refrigerator and let it come to room temperature.

2. **Heat** the oven (with two oven racks toward the middle) to 350°F. **Line** 2 rimmed sheet pans with parchment paper.

3. In a medium bowl, **measure** and **whisk** together the flours,* baking soda, baking powder, and salt.

4. In a large mixing bowl, **combine** the butter, brown sugar, and granulated sugar and **beat** with an electric mixer on medium-high speed (or by hand with a wooden spoon) until fluffy, 2 to 3 minutes, scraping down the sides with a silicone spatula as necessary. **Stop** the mixer; **add** the egg and vanilla, then **beat** in. **Scrape** down the sides. With the mixer on low speed, **use** a large spoon to gradually **add** the flour mixture, and **mix** until just incorporated. **Stir** in the chocolate chips.

5. **Drop** the dough in 2-T. balls 2 inches apart onto the prepared pans. **Bake,** rotating the pans 180° halfway through, until the edges are golden brown and set (the center will still be quite soft), 14 to 18 minutes. **Let cool** on the pan 5 minutes before transferring to a wire rack. **Repeat** with the remaining dough.

6. Once cool, **store** in an airtight container for up to 4 days.

# Oatmeal, Maple & Raisin Cookies

An old-fashioned crispy-chewy-sweet treat. My man Jerry Seinfeld is all over these.

8 tablespoons (1 stick)
   unsalted butter
1 c. all-purpose flour
½ tsp. ground cinnamon
¼ tsp. baking soda
¼ tsp. kosher salt
¾ c. sugar
1 large egg
1 T. maple syrup
1¼ c. old-fashioned
   rolled oats
½ c. golden raisins

Tools needed: 2 rimmed sheet pans, parchment paper, medium bowl, whisk, large mixing bowl, electric mixer, wooden spoon, measuring cups and spoons, silicone spatula, large spoon, kitchen timer, metal spatula, wire rack.

**\*** How-to:
   Measure flour, p. 42

Don't Panic: Using an electric mixer may put you off, but it's only about as complicated as using a blow-dryer. Use medium-high speed for beating the butter and sugar, but have it on low speed when you add the flour so you avoid making a crazy mess.

1. At least an hour beforehand, **take** the butter out of the refrigerator and let it come to room temperature.

2. **Heat** the oven (with two oven racks toward the middle) to 350°F. **Line** 2 rimmed sheet pans with parchment paper.

3. In a medium bowl, **measure** and **whisk** together the flour,**\*** cinnamon, baking soda, and salt.

4. In a large mixing bowl, **combine** the butter and sugar and **beat** with an electric mixer on medium-high speed (or by hand with a wooden spoon) until fluffy, 2 to 3 minutes, scraping down the sides with a silicone spatula as necessary. **Stop** the mixer; **add** the egg and maple syrup, then **beat** in. **Scrape** down the sides. With the mixer on low speed, **use** a large spoon to gradually **add** the flour mixture and **mix** until just incorporated. **Stir** in the oats and raisins.

5. **Drop** the dough in 1 T.-size mounds 2 inches apart onto the prepared pans. **Bake**, rotating the pans 180° halfway through, until light golden brown, 12 to 15 minutes. **Let cool** on the pan 5 minutes before transferring to a wire rack.

6. Once cool, **store** in an airtight container for up to 4 days.

# DROPS

These are heavenly. Made in the food processor, these no-bake cookies are wheat-free/dairy-free/vegan.

Don't Panic: These are a no-brainer, once you are comfortable with that food processor. (DO IT!)

### CHOCOLATE CHIA DROPS

1 c. (packed full) pitted dates (Deglet or Medjool)
½ c. raisins
½ c. semisweet chocolate chips
¼ c. unsweetened shredded coconut
¼ c. almond butter
1 T. coconut oil
1½ c. crispy brown rice cereal
2 T. chia seeds

**Place** the dates, raisins, and chocolate in a food processor and **pulse** several times until finely chopped.* **Add** the coconut, almond butter, and coconut oil and **pulse** until evenly combined. **Add** the cereal and chia seeds and **give** it a few quick mini pulses only to combine (you don't want to completely crush the cereal). Using the palms of your hands, **form** into small, two-bite-size drops. **Store** in an airtight container for up to 5 days.

Tools needed: food processor, measuring cups and spoons.

\* How-to: Use a food processor, p. 16

### PEANUT BUTTER DROPS

1½ c. (packed full) pitted dates (Deglet or Medjool)
½ c. roasted peanuts
½ c. unsweetened shredded coconut
½ c. peanut butter
1 T. coconut oil
2 tsp. ground cinnamon
¼ tsp. kosher salt
1 c. crispy brown rice cereal

**Place** the dates in a food processor and **pulse** until finely chopped.* **Add** the peanuts, coconut, peanut butter, coconut oil, cinnamon, and salt and **pulse** until chopped but not finely chopped. **Add** the cereal and **give** it a few quick mini pulses only to combine (you don't want to completely crush the cereal). Using the palms of your hands, **form** into small, two-bite-size drops. **Store** in an airtight container for up to 5 days.

### CHERRY-GINGER-ALMOND DROPS

1 c. (packed full) pitted dates (Deglet or Medjool)
1 c. dried cherries
⅓ c. sliced candied ginger
½ c. plus ¼ c. unsweetened shredded coconut
⅓ c. raw almonds
¼ c. almond butter
1 T. coconut oil
¼ tsp. kosher salt
1½ c. crispy brown rice cereal

**Place** the dates, cherries, and ginger in a food processor and **pulse** until finely chopped.* **Add** ½ c. of the coconut, the almonds, almond butter, coconut oil, and salt and **pulse** until chopped but not finely chopped. **Add** the cereal and **give** it a few quick mini pulses only to combine (you don't want to completely crush the cereal). Using the palms of your hands, **form** into small, two-bite-size drops. **Roll** in the remaining ¼ c. coconut. **Store** in an airtight container for up to 5 days.

# Flourless Fudge Cake with Whipped Cream

Get out your whisk—it's time to party. This cake is gluten-free, rich, moist, and delish. And the brandy only adds to the fun.

Cooking spray
8 oz. semisweet chocolate
 or 1¼ c. semisweet
 chocolate chips
12 T. (1½ sticks) unsalted
 butter
2 T. brandy
5 large eggs
1 c. sugar
¾ c. almond flour/meal
Whipped Cream

**WHIPPED CREAM**
2 c. heavy (whipping) cream
¼ c. confectioners' sugar

Tools needed: 9-inch springform or regular cake pan, cutting board, serrated knife (optional), medium saucepan, whisk, measuring cups and spoons, large bowl, silicone spatula, rimmed sheet pan, toothpick, kitchen timer, wire rack, paring knife.

Don't Panic: Make sure the butter and chocolate are melted and well combined before you go to the next step.

1. **Heat** the oven (with the oven rack in the middle) to 325°F. **Coat** the cake pan with cooking spray. If your chocolate is in a block, **chop** (a serrated knife works well) into small pieces.

2. **Place** a medium saucepan on the stove. **Add** the butter and **turn** the heat to medium. Once it's melted, **add** the chocolate, **remove** from the heat, and **whisk** until melted and smooth. **Whisk** in the brandy.

3. In a large bowl, **whisk** together the eggs until an even yellow, then **whisk** in the sugar. Using a silicone spatula, **scrape** the chocolate into the eggs. **Whisk** until incorporated. **Whisk** in the almond flour.

4. **Scrape** the batter into the prepared pan and **place** on a rimmed sheet pan. **Bake** until the middle is set and a toothpick inserted into the center still has a few moist crumbs attached, 40 to 50 minutes. The top will crack; this is normal!

5. **Let cool** completely in the pan on a wire rack. Then **run** a paring knife around the edge and **remove** the metal ring (if using a spring-form pan). **Serve** at room temperature with whipped cream.

**WHIPPED CREAM**
**Pour** the cream into a large bowl. Using a whisk, **whip** the cream with rapid, wide strokes. When it starts to thicken, **add** the sugar. **Continue** to whip only until the whipped cream holds its shape when you lift the whisk out of the bowl.

ACTUAL WORK TIME: 10 minutes | TOTAL TIME: 10 minutes | SERVES: 4

# BROILED HONEY-NUT BANANAS

Oh . . . these. My favorite recipe in the book. I could definitely eat them every night. They have a brittle type of topping that is totally addictive.

½ c. walnut halves
½ c. sliced almonds
2 T. dark brown sugar
2 T. honey
¼ tsp. salt
2 T. unsalted butter
4 bananas

Tools needed: cutting board, chef's knife, medium bowl, measuring cups and spoons, rimmed sheet pan.

* How-to:
Chop nuts, p. 37

Don't Panic: Do not take your beady eyes off these while they broil. The honey can burn quickly.

1. **Heat** the broiler (with the oven rack about 4 inches from the top). **Chop** the walnuts* and **add** to a medium bowl along with the almonds, brown sugar, honey, and salt. **Stir** together. **Cut** the butter into small pieces and **add** to the bowl. Use your fingers to **break** the butter into very small pieces and **combine** with the nut mixture.

2. **Peel** the bananas and **slice** them in half lengthwise. **Place** them, cut side up, on a rimmed sheet pan. **Crumble** the nut mixture over each half. **Broil** until the nuts are golden brown, 1 to 2 minutes.

ACTUAL WORK TIME: 5 minutes | TOTAL TIME: 25 minutes | SERVES: 4

# Marinated Strawberries with Ice Cream

My twelve-year-old daughter, Sascha, makes this for us (with a little help in zesting). You can substitute your favorite fruit and even add lime zest or freshly grated ginger. The fruit gets juicy and saucy, and is a spectacular topping for your favorite vanilla ice cream.

1 lb. strawberries
2 T. sugar
Grated zest of 1 lemon (about 1 tsp.)
1 T. lemon juice
1 pint vanilla ice cream

Tools needed: cutting board, paring knife, medium bowl, measuring spoons, grater/zester, citrus juicer, ice cream scoop.

* How-to:
Zest citrus, p. 24
Juice citrus, p. 25

Don't Panic: Nothing happens here that even the most terrified can't handle.

1. **Wash** the strawberries. Using your paring knife, **cut off** the stems. Then **cut** the strawberries in half or into quarters if they are large. **Put** them in a medium bowl.

2. **Sprinkle** the sugar over the berries and **grate** in the lemon zest.* **Juice** ½ of the lemon, **add**, and **stir** to combine.* **Let marinate** for at least 20 minutes or overnight. **Spoon** the strawberries and their juice over ice cream.

# Mixed Berry Crisp

This is a year-round dessert that all beginners can learn how to make effortlessly. Use high-quality frozen berries if fresh are not available.

¾ c. packed dark brown sugar

¾ c. old-fashioned rolled oats

½ c. sliced almonds

½ tsp. ground or grated whole nutmeg (about 25 passes on a grater)

¼ tsp. kosher salt

½ c. plus 2 T. whole wheat flour

6 T. cold unsalted butter

8 c. mixed berries, such as blueberries, blackberries, and raspberries (fresh or frozen)

¼ c. granulated sugar

Vanilla ice cream, for serving (optional, but recommended!)

**Tools needed:** medium bowl, large bowl, measuring cups and spoons, cutting board, paring knife, 2- to 2½-qt. baking dish, rimmed sheet pan, grater/zester, kitchen timer.

**\* How-to:**
  Measure flour, p. 42

Don't Panic: Using your fingers to combine the crisp topping is actually fun.

1. **Heat** the oven (with the oven rack in the middle) to 350°F.

2. In a medium bowl, **combine** the brown sugar, oats, almonds, nutmeg, salt, and ½ c. of the flour\* and **mix** together. **Cut** the butter into small pieces, **add** to the bowl, and, using your fingertips, **squeeze** and **combine** until the mixture resembles coarse crumbs. This is your crisp topping.

3. In a large bowl, **toss** together the berries, granulated sugar, and the remaining 2 T. flour. **Pour** into the baking dish. **Sprinkle** the crisp topping over the berries, squeezing it into small clumps as you go. **Place** the dish on a rimmed sheet pan and **transfer** to the oven. **Bake** until the top is crisp and golden brown and the berries are bubbling, 40 to 45 minutes. **Serve** warm or at room temperature with vanilla ice cream, if you please.

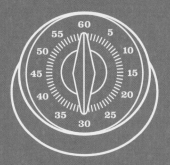

# QUICKIES

There are some of you who don't feel ready to cook a full-on meal yet. That's fine. You can start here with some quick, no-fail (and even good for you), simple fare. I know you can handle these. Getting comfortable in your kitchen is a big first step. These are a nice way to find your way into cooking. These are not life-changing, revolutionary ideas—but they hopefully feel accessible and even inspiring to you. Breakfast and lunch are not the easiest times to get creative or courageous. And it's very easy to get into a rut or pattern that doesn't always make the most sense for your health and pocketbook. Sometimes you just need some ideas . . . I hope these work for you.

# Breakfast

### Make-It-Yourself Muesli
### (2 generous servings)

Roughly chop ¼ c. **raw almonds** (p. 37)
and place in a bowl. Add ½ c. **old-
fashioned rolled oats**, ¼ c. **dried
cherries**, ¼ c. **shredded coconut**,
and 1 T. **brown sugar.** Using a cheese
grater, grate ½ of an **apple** into the
bowl. Mix and divide. Serve with your
favorite kind of **milk.**

### Cottage Cheese &
### Pomegranate Seeds

Cut a **pomegranate** into quarters. Over
a large bowl, slide your thumb under
the seeds to force them out. Pick out
any white membranes. Spread a **Wasa
cracker** with **cottage cheese** and
scatter **pomegranate seeds** over the
top. Drizzle with **honey.**

## English Muffin with Peanut Butter, Banana & Coconut

Split a **whole wheat English muffin** in half and toast to golden brown. Spread with **peanut** or **almond butter**, then layer with **sliced banana.** Sprinkle with **shredded coconut** and **cinnamon.**

## Strawberries with Yogurt & Balsamic

Quarter some **strawberries** (take the stem off first). Spoon some **Greek yogurt** into a bowl and add the **strawberries** and a drizzle of **balsamic vinegar** to your liking. Grate whole **nutmeg** over the top.

## Avocado Toast

Toast a slice of **sourdough bread.**
Slice ½ of an **avocado** in its skin
(page 35). Scoop out and spread over
the toast. Squeeze some **lemon** over
the top and sprinkle with **salt** and
**crushed red pepper.** P.S.—You can
skip the bread and eat the
avocado out of its skin with the
same preparation.

## Broiled Grapefruit with Almonds & Honey (2 servings)

Heat the broiler (with the oven rack
about 4 inches from the top). On
your cutting board, thinly slice both
ends off the **grapefruit.** Then cut
the grapefruit in half. With each half
resting evenly, use the tip of a paring
knife to slice around each section
to make for easy eating. Place on
a rimmed sheet pan. Sprinkle with
**sliced almonds** and drizzle with
**honey.** Broil a few minutes until the
almonds are golden brown.

## Tomato & Ricotta on Toast

Thinly slice a **tomato** into rounds. Toast a slice of **whole wheat bread,** then spread with **fresh ricotta cheese.** Top with **tomato slices, dried oregano, salt, pepper,** and a drizzle of **olive oil.** If you feel comfortable, you can then broil this so it's hot and "melt-y."

## Blueberry-Almond Smoothie (2 servings)

In a blender, combine 1½ cups **frozen blueberries,** 1 **banana,** ¼ cup **plain yogurt,** 3 T. **almond butter,** and ¼ cup **coconut water.** Blend until smooth.

# Lunches & Dinners

## Rice Cake with Cucumbers & Salsa

Spread a **rice cake** with a layer of
**cream cheese** and top with **sprouts**,
sliced **cucumber**, and **fresh salsa**.

## Feta & Bean Flatbread

Crumble some **feta** over a **whole wheat pita** and
warm in the oven. Once the feta is melt-y, **top
with butterbeans** (drained and rinsed), sliced **red
onion** (page 29), halved **grape tomatoes**, **dried
oregano**, **salt**, **pepper**, and a drizzle of **olive oil**.

## Apple-Cheddar Melt

Spread **strawberry jam** on 2 slices of
**sourdough bread**. Sandwich with thinly
sliced **apple** and **Cheddar**. Melt **butter**
in a skillet over medium heat and cook
the sandwich; cover the pan. When
golden brown on the first side, flip and
cook until golden brown on the other
side and the cheese is melted.

## Arugula, Dates, Blue Cheese & Almonds

Top some fresh **arugula** with sliced **dates**,
chopped **almonds,** and crumbled **blue
cheese.** Sprinkle with **salt** and **pepper** and
drizzle with **olive oil.**

## Cottage Cheese–Stuffed Avocado with Hot Sauce

Cut an **avocado** in half and remove the pit. Fill each half with **cottage cheese** and top with **hot sauce**.

## Prosciutto, Pear & Parmesan

Arrange thinly sliced **prosciutto** with **pear** wedges and **Parmesan** pieces on a plate. Top with some **olive oil** and **pepper**.

## Tuna & Apple Pita Pizza

Split a **whole wheat pita** in half. Brush the cut side of each round with **olive oil** and broil until crisp. Top with fresh **spinach**, **canned albacore tuna**, sliced **apple**, and grated **Gruyère** or **Swiss cheese**. Broil again until the cheese melts.

## Sliced Tomato & Egg Open-Faced Sandwich

Layer a slice of **light rye bread** with **sliced tomato**, **hard-boiled egg**, and **dill pickle**. Top with **salt, pepper,** and a drizzle of **olive oil.** (For perfect hard-boiled eggs, place them in a saucepan and cover with cold water by 2 inches. Bring to a boil, remove from the heat, cover, and let stand for 12 minutes. Drain and transfer to a bowl of ice water to cool. Good for 1 week, unpeeled, in the fridge.)

OTHER
USEFUL
THINGS

# What's in Season?

We are constantly hearing about eating locally and in season. You've probably heard many times how beneficial it is for your body and the environment. I wholeheartedly support and agree with this philosophy. But I also know that it is not always easy or even possible to do that! If you can shop at local farmers' markets and stores that carry local produce, it's a wonderful thing. If you can't, below is a general guide for you to keep in mind when you do shop. Try to at least keep it in season—that way you know you are more likely to be getting the most flavor and freshness possible. All this being said, I'm a big fan of also using frozen organic veggies.

| SPRING: | SUMMER: | FALL: | WINTER: | YEAR-ROUND: |
|---|---|---|---|---|
| apricots | bell peppers | apples | acorn squash | bananas |
| artichokes | berries | broccoli | cabbage | beets |
| asparagus | chard | brussels sprouts | collard greens | carrots |
| cherries | corn | butternut squash | grapefruit | celery |
| new potatoes | cucumbers | cauliflower | kale | fennel |
| peas | eggplant | grapes | oranges | garlic |
| radishes | figs | parsnips | pineapple | lemons |
| rhubarb | green beans | pears | turnips | limes |
| strawberries | melons | persimmons | | mushrooms |
| sugar snap peas | nectarines | pomegranates | | onions |
| | okra | sweet potatoes | | potatoes |
| | peaches | | | shallots |
| | plums | | | spinach |
| | tomatoes | | | |
| | zucchini | | | |

# Meat Temperature Chart

Meat can be a very easy thing to learn how to cook. In my opinion, the hardest part of grilling, broiling, or roasting meat is knowing when it's done. I don't love to need lots of gadgets, and I try to make do with what I have. However, when it comes to cooking meat, an instant-read thermometer has improved my kitchen life dramatically. I highly recommend purchasing one if you're a carnivore. It's inexpensive and worth getting.

**TO USE:** After the specified cooking time, check that your meat or poultry is done by inserting the thermometer into the thickest part of the roast (without touching the bone). For steaks, chops, and chicken breasts, insert it through the side to reach the middle. Check the chart to the right with my recommendations for doneness (please note that for beef and lamb, my suggestions are a few degrees less than what the USDA recommends). And remember, always let your cooked meat rest 5 to 10 minutes before slicing.

## BEEF & LAMB
Rare: 115°–120°F
Medium-rare: 125°–130°F
Medium: 135°–140°F
Medium-well: 145°–150°F
Well-done: 155°–160°F
Ground: 160°F

## PORK
Medium: 145°F
Ground: 160°F

## POULTRY
Thighs, legs, wings, and ground: 165°F
Breasts: 160°F

## OVEN TEMPERATURES

| Fahrenheit | Celsius | British Gas Mark | French Gas Setting |
|---|---|---|---|
| 250° | 120° | ½ | 3 |
| 275° | 135° | 1 | 3 |
| 300° | 150° | 2 | 4 |
| 325° | 165° | 3 | 4 |
| 350° | 175° | 4 | 4 |
| 375° | 190° | 5 | 5 |
| 400° | 200° | 6 | 5 |
| 425° | 220° | 7 | 6 |
| 450° | 230° | 8 | 6 |
| 475° | 245° | 9 | |

Celsius to Fahrenheit: multiply Celsius by 1.8, then add 32.
Fahrenheit to Celsius: subtract 32 from Fahrenheit, then multiply by 0.5556.

# Storage Guidelines & Food Safety Pointers

Sometimes it's more convenient to do a big shop and get lots of ingredients at one time. It's important to know how long items will keep fresh in your refrigerator or freezer. It's also wise to keep your eye on your leftovers. As a general rule, don't keep leftovers for more than 4 days, but below is a chart you might find helpful.

| FOOD | REFRIGERATOR (how long it will last) | FREEZER (how long it will last) |
| --- | --- | --- |
| **BEEF & LAMB (RAW)** | | |
| Roasts and chops | 3 days | 6 months |
| Ground | 2 days | 4 months |
| Sausage (uncooked) | 2 days | 2 months |
| **POULTRY (RAW)** | | |
| Whole and pieces | 2 days | 6 months |
| Ground | 2 days | 4 months |
| **PORK (RAW)** | | |
| Roasts and chops | 3 days | 6 months |
| Bacon | 1 week (opened); 2 weeks (unopened) | 1 month |
| Sausage (uncooked) | 2 days | 2 months |
| **SEAFOOD (RAW)** | | |
| Fish | 2 days | 4 months |
| Shrimp | 1 day | 4 months |
| Clams, mussels, oysters | 1 day | don't freeze |
| **DELI & CURED MEATS** | | |
| Sliced lunchmeat | 4 days | 2 months |
| Hot dogs | 1 week | 2 months |
| **LEFTOVERS** | | |
| Soups, stews, chili | 4 days | 3 months |
| Casseroles | 4 days | 3 months |
| Meat and poultry | 3 days | 2 months |
| Fish | 2 days | don't freeze |
| Most other leftovers | 4 days | don't freeze |

## HOW TO STORE IN THE REFRIGERATOR

- Store raw meats, poultry, fish, and deli meats in their original packaging on the bottom shelf of your refrigerator. To be on the safe side, place them in separate ziptop bags to prevent any juices from escaping.

- Store leftovers in airtight containers or ziptop bags to seal in freshness and keep refrigerator odors out.

## HOW TO FREEZE

- Cool cooked items to room temperature before freezing.

- Freeze in small portions (for fast freezing and thawing).

- When freezing soups or sauces in containers, leave about ½ inch at the top for expansion.

- Use bags and containers made for the freezer. When using bags, squeeze out all of the air. When using plastic wrap or foil, double- or triple-wrap. You can freeze in the original unopened packaging, but wrap again with plastic wrap or foil for extra protection.

- Be sure to label your items and include the date.

## HOW TO THAW

- Preferred method: Thaw overnight in the refrigerator (or figure 8 hours per pound of meat to thaw).

- Or you can completely submerge the item (wrapped) in a large bowl of cold water (not warm or hot water because you don't want your food to get warmer than 40°F) and change the water every 30 minutes for a maximum of 2 hours.

- Or you can defrost in the microwave at 1- or 2-minute intervals on the defrost setting, checking your food each time to make sure it's not cooking. If you use the microwave to defrost, cook the food immediately, as the microwave heats unevenly and some parts might be warm or partially cooked.

## FOOD SAFETY POINTERS

1 Wash your hands with warm, soapy water before and after handling food.

2 Always wash hands, knives, cutting boards, and faucet handles with hot, soapy water after they come in contact with raw, poultry, meat, and fish.

3 Run sponges through the dishwasher often or replace them frequently.

4 Always keep raw poultry, meat, or fish separate and away from fresh vegetables and prepared foods.

5 Always wash the plate or cutting board that held raw poultry, meat, or fish before you reuse it.

6 Always marinate food in the refrigerator, not on the counter. Throw out the used marinade.

7 Let foods cool to room temperature first before refrigerating or freezing.

8 Don't let food sit out on the counter longer than 2 hours.

# Measurement Conversions & Equivalents

## SOME USEFUL U.S. MEASUREMENT EQUIVALENTS

| | |
|---|---|
| 3 tsp. | = 1 T. |
| 4 T. | = ½ c.; 2 fluid oz. |
| 5 T. + 1 tsp. | = ⅓ c. |
| 8 T. | = ½ c.; 4 fluid oz. |
| 16 T. | = 1 c.; 8 fluid oz. |
| 2 c. | = 1 pt.; 16 fluid oz. |
| 4 c. | = 1 qt.; 32 fluid oz. |
| 2 pt. | = 1 qt.; 32 fluid oz. |
| 4 qt. | = 1 gal.; 8 pt. |
| 1 lb. (pound) | = 16 oz. |

## METRIC CONVERSION FORMULAS

| To Convert | Multiply |
|---|---|
| oz. to grams | oz. by 28.35 |
| lb. to kilograms | lb. by .454 |
| tsp. to milliliters | tsp. by 4.93 |
| T. to milliliters | T. by 14.79 |
| fluid oz. to milliliters | fluid oz. by 29.57 |
| c. to milliliters | c. by 236.59 |
| c. to liters | c. by .236 |
| pt. to liters | pt. by .473 |
| qt. to liters | qt. by .946 |
| gal. to liters | gal. by 3.785 |
| inches to centimeters | inches by 2.54 |

## SOME COMMON INGREDIENT WEIGHTS

| Measurement | Grams |
|---|---|
| 1 c. all-purpose flour | = 125 |
| 1 c. whole wheat flour | = 120 |
| 1 stick butter (½ c.; 8 T.) | = 113 |
| 1 c. firmly packed brown sugar | = 225 |
| 1 c. granulated sugar | = 200 |
| 1 tsp. baking powder | = 3.5 |
| 1 tsp. baking soda | = 4.6 |

## APPROXIMATE METRIC EQUIVALENTS

### Weight

| | |
|---|---|
| ¼ oz. | = 7 grams |
| ½ oz. | = 14 grams |
| ¾ oz. | = 21 grams |
| 1 oz. | = 28 grams |
| 1½ oz. | = 42.5 grams |
| 2 oz. | = 57 grams |
| 3 oz. | = 85 grams |
| 4 oz. (¼ lb.) | = 113 grams |
| 5 oz. | = 142 grams |
| 6 oz. | = 170 grams |
| 7 oz. | = 198 grams |
| 8 oz. (½ lb.) | = 227 grams |
| 16 oz. (1 lb.) | = 454 grams |
| 35.25 oz. (2.2 lb.) | = 1 kilogram |

### Volume

| | |
|---|---|
| ¼ tsp. | = 1 milliliter |
| ½ tsp. | = 2.5 milliliters |
| ¾ tsp. | = 4 milliliters |
| 1 tsp. | = 5 milliliters |
| 1¼ tsp. | = 6 milliliters |
| 1½ tsp. | = 7.5 milliliters |
| 1¾ tsp. | = 8.5 milliliters |
| 2 tsp. | = 10 milliliters |
| 1 T. (½ fluid oz.) | = 15 milliliters |
| 2 T. (1 fluid oz.) | = 30 milliliters |
| ¼ c. | = 59 milliliters |
| ⅓ c. | = 79 milliliters |
| ½ c. (4 fluid oz.) | = 118 milliliters |
| ⅔ c. | = 158 milliliters |
| ¾ c. | = 180 milliliters |
| 1 c. (8 fluid oz.) | = 240 milliliters |
| 1½ c. (12 fluid oz.) | = 350 milliliters |
| 2 c. (1 pt.) | = 475 milliliters |
| 3 c. | = 710 milliliters |
| 4 c. (1 qt.) | = 0.95 liter |
| 1 qt. plus ¼ c. | = 1 liter |
| 4 qt. (1 gal.) | = 3.8 liters |

# NOTES

# Index

(Page numbers in *italic* refer to illustrations. Page numbers with *f* refer to the foldout following that page.)

## A

abbreviations, 3
acorn squash, 229
almond(s):
    Arugula, Dates, Blue Cheese &, 225, *225*
    Blueberry Smoothie, 223, *223*
    Broiled Grapefruit with Honey &, 222, *222*
    Broiled Honey-Nut Bananas, *212*, 213
    butter, in Chocolate Chia Drops, *208*, 209
    -Cherry-Ginger Drops, *208*, 209
    Freaky Greek Pasta, *126*, 127
    Green Beans with, *148*, 149
    Mixed Berry Crisp, *216*, 217
    Muesli, Make-It-Yourself, 220, *220*
    Toasted, Tomato & Watermelon Salad with, *198*, 199
    toasting, 37
apple(s), 229
    Cheddar Melt, 225, *225*
    Chicken Salad with Basil, *200*, 201
    Cider Pork Chops, *102*, 103
    Muesli, Make-It-Yourself, 220, *220*
    Pork Loin with Onions &, *100*, 101
    & Tuna Pita Pizza, 227, *227*
appliances 16–17, *16–17*
apricots, 229
artichokes, 229
arugula:

Crispy Chicken Cutlets with Lemon &, *76*, 77
Dates, Blue Cheese, & Almonds, 225, *225*
asparagus, 229
    buying & storing, 155
    Roasted, with Lemon, *154*, 155
avocado, 34–35
    Cottage Cheese–Stuffed, with Hot Sauce, 226, *226*
    Guacamole, 93*f*
    prepping, 34
    scooping, 34
    slicing & dicing, 35
    Toast, 222, *222*

## B

bacon:
    Stir-fried Rice with Sunny-side Up Eggs, *188*, 189
    -Wrapped Meat Loaf, *98*, 99
Baked Egg Noodles & Cheese, *130*, 131
bakeware, *11*, 15
baking pans, *11*, 15
banana(s), 229
    Blueberry-Almond Smoothie, 223, *223*
    Broiled Honey-Nut, *212*, 213
    Date Bran Muffins, *60*, 61
    English Muffin with Peanut Butter, Coconut &, 221, *221*
Barbecue Chicken, *82*, 83
basil, 32
    Chicken Salad with Apples &, *200*, 201
    Pesto Pasta, *140*, 141
    Pizza Margherita, *142*, 143
Bass, Bread Crumb, *112*, 113
bean(s):
    Cannellini, Garlic & Rosemary, *186*, 187
    Chickpeas, Couscous Salad with Tomatoes, Mint &, *184*, 185

& Feta Flatbread, 224, *224*
kidney, in Your First Chili, *96*, 97
refried, in Huevos Rancheros, *54*, 55
White, Stewy Shrimp with Tomatoes, *120*, 121
*see also* green beans
beef, 87–99
    Chili, Your First, *96*, 97
    Chili-Rubbed Skirt Steak Tacos (with Salsa & Guacamole), *92*, 93
    Hamburger, the Most Simple, Broiled, Perfect, *94*, 95
    Herb-Roasted, with Potatoes & Carrots, *90*, 91
    internal temperature & doneness of, 231
    Meat Loaf, Bacon-Wrapped, *98*, 99
    patting dry before cooking, 43
    Peppercorn Steak, Simple, *88*, 89
    storage guidelines for, 232
beets, 229
berry(ies), 229
    Fresh, Crumb Cake, *62*, 63
    Mixed, Crisp, *216*, 217
    *see also* strawberries
blenders, *17*
Blueberry-Almond Smoothie, 223, *223*
blue cheese:
    Arugula, Dates, Almonds &, 225, *225*
    Warm Spinach Salad with, *196*, 197
Bolognese, Turkey, *128*, 129
bowls, mixing, *10*, 14
Bran Muffins, Banana-Date, *60*, 61
Bread Crumb Bass, *112*, 113
breakfast, 45–63
    Banana-Date Bran Muffins, *60*, 61

Fresh Berry Crumb Cake, *62*, 63

Fried Eggs over Broiled Tomatoes, *48*, 49

Huevos Rancheros, *54*, 55

Lemon Ricotta Pancakes, *58*, 59

Scrambled Eggs & Cream Cheese, *46*, 47

Shepherd's French Toast, *56*, 57

Soft-boiled Eggs with Toast a.k.a. The Granny Egg, *50*, 51

Stir-fried Rice with Sunny-side Up Eggs, *188*, 189

Sweet Pea & Onion Frittata, *52*, 53

breakfast quickies, 220–23

Avocado Toast, 222, *222*

Blueberry-Almond Smoothie, 223, *223*

Cottage Cheese & Pomegranate Seeds, 220, *220*

English Muffin with Peanut Butter, Banana, & Coconut, 221, *221*

Grapefruit, Broiled, with Almonds & Honey, 222, *222*

Muesli, Make-It-Yourself, 220, *220*

Strawberries with Yogurt & Balsamic, 221, *221*

Tomato & Ricotta on Toast, 223, *223*

broccoli, 229

buying & storing, 147

Freaky Greek Pasta, *126*, 127

with Golden Raisins & Garlic, *146*, 147

broiled:

Grapefruit with Almonds & Honey, 222, *222*

Hamburger, the Most Simple, Perfect, *94*, 95

Honey-Nut Bananas, *212*, 213

Lamb Chops with Mint Jelly, *104*, 105

brown rice:

cereal, crispy, in Drops (Chocolate Chia Drops, Peanut Butter Drops, & Cherry-Ginger-Almond Drops), *208*, 209

cooking, 189

Pilaf, *178*, 179

Bruschetta, Summer Tomato, *170*, 171

Brussels sprouts, 229

buying & storing, 161

Roasted, *160*, 161

Bulgur Wheat Pilaf, Sweet Pea, *180*, 181

butterbeans, in Feta & Bean Flatbread, 224, *224*

Butter Lettuce Salad with Pine Nuts & Parsley, *194*, 195

butternut squash, 229

C

cabbage, 229

Cacio e Pepe, *136*, 137

Caesar Vinaigrette, 193*f*

cake pans, *11*, 15

cakes:

Flourless Fudge, with Whipped Cream, *210*, 211

Fresh Berry Crumb, *62*, 63

Cannellini Beans, Garlic & Rosemary, *186*, 187

can openers, *12*, 14

carrot(s), 36, 229

buying & storing, 163*f*

chopping, 36

Fries, 163*f*

Garlic & Rosemary Cannellini Beans, *186*, 187

Herb-Roasted Beef with Potatoes &, *90*, 91

sticks, making, 36

cauliflower, 229

buying & storing, 159

Roasted, & Sage, *158*, 159

celery, 229

cereal:

crispy brown rice, in Drops (Chocolate Chia Drops, Peanut Butter Drops, & Cherry-Ginger-Almond Drops), *208*, 209

Muesli, Make-It-Yourself, 220, *220*

chard, 229

Cheddar:

Apple Melt, 225, *225*

Baked Egg Noodles & Cheese, *130*, 131

cheese:

Baked Egg Noodles &, *130*, 131

Blue, Arugula, Dates, Almonds &, 225, *225*

Blue, Warm Spinach Salad with, *196*, 197

Cheddar-Apple Melt, 225, *225*

Cottage, & Pomegranate Seeds, 220, *220*

Cottage, –Stuffed Avocado with Hot Sauce, 226, *226*

Cream, Scrambled Eggs &, *46*, 47

feta, in Freaky Greek Pasta, *126*, 127

Feta & Bean Flatbread, 224, *224*

mozzarella, in Pizza Margherita, *142*, 143

pecorino, in Cacio e Pepe, *136*, 137

Slow-Cooker Lasagna, *134*, 135

*see also* Parmesan; ricotta

cherry(ies), 229

dried, in Make-It-Yourself Muesli, 220, *220*

-Ginger-Almond Drops, *208*, 209

Chia Chocolate Drops, *208*, 209

chicken, 65–85
   Breasts, Pan-Roasted, *66*, 67
   Cutlets, Crispy, with Arugula &
      Lemon, *76*, 77
   Drumsticks, Roasted–4 Easy
      Recipes! (Barbecue Chick-
      en, Mustard & Rosemary
      Chicken, Yogurt & Cumin
      Chicken, Lemon & Sage
      Chicken), *82*, 83
   Fast & Juicy Herb-Grilled, *74*, 75
   Parm, 77*f*
   with Rice & Peas, *70*, 71
   Roast, Seriously Basic, *84*, 85
   Roasted Sweet Potatoes, Toma-
      toes &, *78*, 79
   Rosemary, Under a "Brick,"
      *72*, 73
   Salad with Apples & Basil,
      *200*, 201
   Skillet-Roasted Potatoes &,
      *68*, 69
   washing, 43
   Wings, Sweet & Spicy, *80*, 81
Chickpeas, Couscous Salad with
   Tomatoes, Mint &, *184*, 185
Chili, Your First, *96*, 97
Chili-Rubbed Skirt Steak Tacos
   (with Salsa & Guacamole),
   *92*, 93
Chips, Kale, *174*, 175
Chives, Smashed Red Potatoes
   with, *152*, 153
chocolate:
   Chia Drops, *208*, 209
   Chip Cookies, *204*, 205
   Flourless Fudge Cake with
      Whipped Cream, *210*, 211
Cider, Apple, Pork Chops, *102*, 103
cilantro, 32
citrus, 24–25
   zesting or juicing, 19, 24–25
   *see also* grapefruit; lemon(s);
      lime(s)
citrus juicers, *13*, 15

Clams, Pasta with, Slammin', *138*,
   139
coconut:
   Drops (Chocolate Chia Drops,
      Peanut Butter Drops, &
      Cherry-Ginger-Almond
      Drops), *208*, 209
   English Muffin with Peanut
      Butter, Banana &, 221, *221*
   Muesli, Make-It-Yourself, 220,
      *220*
colanders, *10*, 14
collard greens, 229
condiments:
   Guacamole, 93*f*
   Salsa, 93*f*
cookies:
   Chocolate Chip, *204*, 205
   Drops (Chocolate Chia Drops,
      Peanut Butter Drops, &
      Cherry-Ginger-Almond
      Drops), *208*, 209
   Oatmeal, Maple, & Raisin, *206*,
      207
cookware, *8*, 9
corn, 229
   buying & storing, 173
   Mexican, *172*, 173
corn tortillas:
   Chili-Rubbed Skirt Steak Tacos
      (with Salsa & Guacamole),
      *92*, 93
   Huevos Rancheros, *54*, 55
cottage cheese:
   & Pomegranate Seeds, 220,
      *220*
   –Stuffed Avocado with Hot
      Sauce, 226, *226*
Couscous Salad with Chickpeas,
   Tomatoes, & Mint, *184*, 185
Cranberry & Toasted Pine Nut
   Quinoa, *182*, 183
Cream Cheese, Scrambled Eggs
   &, *46*, 47
Crisp, Mixed Berry, *216*, 217

Crispy Chicken Cutlets with Arugula & Lemon, *76*, 77
Crispy Shrimp, *118*, 119
Crumb Cake, Fresh Berry, *62*, 63
cucumbers, 229
   Rice Cake with Salsa &, 224,
      *224*
   Tomato & Watermelon Salad
      with Toasted Almonds, *198*,
      199
Cumin & Yogurt Chicken, *82*, 83
cured meats, storage guidelines
   for, 232
cutting boards, *10*, 14

**D**
date(s):
   Arugula, Blue Cheese, &
      Almonds, 225, *225*
   Banana Bran Muffins, *60*, 61
   Drops (Chocolate Chia Drops,
      Peanut Butter Drops, &
      Cherry-Ginger-Almond
      Drops), *208*, 209
deli meats, storage guidelines for,
   232
desserts, 203–17
   Bananas, Broiled Honey-Nut,
      *212*, 213
   Chocolate Chip Cookies, *204*,
      205
   Drops (Chocolate Chia Drops,
      Peanut Butter Drops, &
      Cherry-Ginger-Almond
      Drops), *208*, 209
   Flourless Fudge Cake with
      Whipped Cream, *210*, 211
   Mixed Berry Crisp, *216*, 217
   Oatmeal, Maple, & Raisin
      Cookies, *206*, 207
   Strawberries, Marinated, with
      Ice Cream, *214*, 215
dinner quickies, *see* lunch or din-
   ner quickies
Drops (Chocolate Chia Drops,

Peanut Butter Drops, & Cherry-Ginger-Almond Drops), *208*, 209

**E**

egg(s):
Fried, over Broiled Tomatoes, *48*, 49
Huevos Rancheros, *54*, 55
Scrambled, & Cream Cheese, *46*, 47
Shepherd's French Toast, *56*, 57
Sliced Tomato &, Open-Faced Sandwich, 227, *227*
Soft-boiled, with Toast a.k.a. The Granny Egg, *50*, 51
Sunny-side Up, Stir-fried Rice with, *188*, 189
Sweet Pea & Onion Frittata, *52*, 53
eggplant, 229
buying & storing, 157
& Cherry Tomatoes, Roasted, *156*, 157
English Muffin with Peanut Butter, Banana, & Coconut, 221, *221*

**F**

fennel, 229
feta:
& Bean Flatbread, 224, *224*
Freaky Greek Pasta, *126*, 127
figs, 229
fish & seafood, 107–21
Bass, Bread Crumb, *112*, 113
checking for doneness, 41
Clams, Slammin' Pasta with, *138*, 139
Halibut, Hoisin, *116*, 117
Halibut over Spinach, Perfect, *114*, 115
Salmon, Succulent Lemon-Thyme, *110*, 111
Seafood Watch, 40
sold with skin on, 41

storage guidelines for, 232
Striped Bass & Tomatoes, Roasted, *108*, 109
Tuna & Apple Pita Pizza, 227, *227*
washing, 43
*see also* shrimp
Flatbread, Feta & Bean, 224, *224*
flour, measuring, 42
Flourless Fudge Cake with Whipped Cream, *210*, 211
food processors, 16, *16*, *17*
food safety pointers, 233
Freaky Greek Pasta, *126*, 127
freezing foods, 233
French Toast, Shepherd's, *56*, 57
Fried Eggs over Broiled Tomatoes, *48*, 49
Fries, Oven (Carrot Fries, Parsnip Fries, & Russet Potato Fries), *162*, 163
Frittata, Sweet Pea & Onion, *52*, 53
fruit:
washing, 43
*see also specific fruits*
Fudge Cake, Flourless, with Whipped Cream, *210*, 211

**G**

garlic, 26–27, 229
chopping, 19, 27
peeling, 27
removing a clove, 26
& Rosemary Cannellini Beans, *186*, 187
smashing, 26
Ginger-Cherry-Almond Drops, *208*, 209
grains, 177–85
Brown Rice Pilaf, *178*, 179
Bulgur Wheat Pilaf, Sweet Pea, *180*, 181
Couscous Salad with Chickpeas, Tomatoes, & Mint, *184*, 185

Quinoa, Toasted Pine Nut & Cranberry, *182*, 183
Rice, Stir-fried, with Sunny-side Up Eggs, *188*, 189
grapefruit, 229
Broiled, with Almonds & Honey, 222, *222*
grapes, 229
graters, *12*, 14
Greek Pasta, Freaky, *126*, 127
green beans, 229
with Almonds, *148*, 149
buying & storing, 149
greens, washing, 43
Grilled Chicken, Herb-, Fast & Juicy, *74*, 75
Guacamole, 93f

**H**

halibut:
Hoisin, *116*, 117
over Spinach, Perfect, *114*, 115
Hamburger, the Most Simple, Broiled, Perfect, *94*, 95
herb(s), 32–33
chopping, 33
-Grilled Chicken, Fast & Juicy, *74*, 75
picking or stripping leaves, 32
-Roasted Beef with Potatoes & Carrots, *90*, 91
storing, 33
Hoisin Halibut, *116*, 117
honey:
Nut Broiled Bananas, *212*, 213
Shallot Vinaigrette, 193f
Huevos Rancheros, *54*, 55

**I**

Ice Cream, Marinated Strawberries with, *214*, 215
instant-read meat thermometers, *12*, 14, 231
Italian cooking:
Chicken Parm, 77f

Italian cooking (continued):
Pizza Margherita, *142*, 143
Sweet Pea & Onion Frittata, *52*, 53
Tomato Bruschetta, Summer, *170*, 171
see also pasta

**K**
kale, 229
buying & storing, 175
Chips, *174*, 175
Salads–3 Easy Recipes! (Toasted Sesame Seed Vinaigrette, Honey-Shallot Vinaigrette, & Caesar Vinaigrette), *192*, 193
washing, 43
kidney beans, in Your First Chili, *96*, 97
knives, 6, 7

**L**
lamb:
Chops, Broiled, with Mint Jelly, *104*, 105
internal temperature & doneness of, 231
patting dry before cooking, 43
storage guidelines for, 232
Lasagna, Slow-Cooker, *134*, 135
leftovers, storage guidelines for, 232
lemon(s), 229
Crispy Chicken Cutlets with Arugula &, *76*, 77
Freaky Greek Pasta, *126*, 127
Ricotta Pancakes, *58*, 59
Roasted Asparagus with, *154*, 155
& Sage Chicken, *82*, 83
Thyme Roasted Portobello Mushrooms, *164*, 165
Thyme Salmon, Succulent, *110*, 111

zesting or juicing, 19, 24–25
lettuce:
Butter, Salad with Pine Nuts & Parsley, *194*, 195
washing, 43
lime(s), 229
Mexican Corn, *172*, 173
zesting or juicing, 24–25
loaf pans, *11*, 15
lunch or dinner quickies, 224–27
Apple-Cheddar Melt, 225, *225*
Arugula, Dates, Blue Cheese, & Almonds, 225, *225*
Cottage Cheese–Stuffed Avocado with Hot Sauce, 226, *226*
Feta & Bean Flatbread, 224, *224*
Prosciutto, Pear, & Parmesan, 226, *226*
Rice Cake with Cucumbers & Salsa, 224, *224*
Sliced Tomato & Egg Open-Faced Sandwich, 227, *227*
Tuna & Apple Pita Pizza, 227, *227*

**M**
Maple, Oatmeal, & Raisin Cookies, *206*, 207
Margherita Pizza, *142*, 143
marinades:
Barbecue, *82*, 83
Lemon & Sage, *82*, 83
Mustard & Rosemary, *82*, 83
Yogurt & Cumin, *82*, 83
marinara:
Pizza Margherita, *142*, 143
Spaghetti, *132*, 133
Marinated Strawberries with Ice Cream, *214*, 215
measurement conversions & equivalents, 234
measuring cups, *3, 10*, 14
measuring spoons, *3, 10*, 14

meat, 87–105
patting dry, 43
see also beef; lamb; pork
Meat Loaf, Bacon-Wrapped, *98*, 99
meat pounders, *13*, 15
meat temperature chart, 231
melons, 229
Watermelon & Tomato Salad with Toasted Almonds, *198*, 199
Melt, Apple-Cheddar, 225, *225*
Mexican cooking, see Tex-Mex & Mexican cooking
microplane grater/zester, *12*, 14
mint(y):
Couscous Salad with Chickpeas, Tomatoes &, *184*, 185
Sugar Snaps, *168*, 169
Mixed Berry Crisp, *216*, 217
mixers, electric, 17
mixing bowls, *10*, 14
mozzarella:
Pizza Margherita, *142*, 143
Slow-Cooker Lasagna, *134*, 135
Muesli, Make-It-Yourself, 220, *220*
Muffins, Banana-Date Bran, *60*, 61
muffin tins, *11*, 15
mushrooms, 229
buying & storing, 165
Portobello, Roasted Lemon-Thyme, *164*, 165
Mustard & Rosemary Chicken, *82*, 83

**N**
nectarines, 229
noodles:
Egg, & Cheese, Baked, *130*, 131
see also pasta
nut(s), 37
chopping, 37
Honey Broiled Bananas, *212*, 213

toasting, 37
see also almond(s)

**O**

oat(meal)(s):
Maple, & Raisin Cookies, *206*,
207
Mixed Berry Crisp, *216*, 217
Muesli, Make-It-Yourself, 220,
*220*
okra, 229
olive oil, 19
onion(s), 28–29, 229
Pork Loin with Apples &, *100*,
101
prepping, 28
slicing or chopping, 29
Sweet Pea Frittata, *52*, 53
openers, *12*, 14
oranges, 229
zesting or juicing, 24–25
organic ingredients, 19
Oven Fries (Carrot Fries, Parsnip
Fries, & Russet Potato Fries),
*162*, 163
oven temperature equivalencies,
231
oven thermometers, *12*, 15

**P**

Pancakes, Lemon Ricotta, *58*, 59
panini presses, *17*
Pan-Roasted Chicken Breasts, *66*,
67
pans, *8*, 9
Parmesan:
Cacio e Pepe, *136*, 137
Chicken Parm, 77*f*
Mexican Corn, *172*, 173
Prosciutto, Pear &, 226, *226*
parsley, 32
Butter Lettuce Salad with Pine
Nuts &, *194*, 195
parsnip(s), 229
buying & storing, 163*f*

Fries, 163*f*
pasta, 123–41
Cacio e Pepe, *136*, 137
with Clams, Slammin', *138*, 139
Egg Noodles & Cheese, Baked,
*130*, 131
Greek, Freaky, *126*, 127
Lasagna, Slow-Cooker, *134*,
135
Pesto, *140*, 141
Spaghetti Marinara, *132*, 133
Sweet Cherry Tomato, *124*, 125
Turkey Bolognese, *128*, 129
pastry brushes, *13*, 15
pea(s), 229
Chicken with Rice &, *70*, 71
Sweet, Bulgur Wheat Pilaf,
*180*, 181
Sweet, Onion Frittata, *52*, 53
see also sugar snap peas
peaches, 229
peanut butter:
Drops, 209
English Muffin with Banana,
Coconut &, 221, *221*
pear(s), 229
Prosciutto, & Parmesan, 226,
*226*
pecorino, in Cacio e Pepe, *136*, 137
peelers, *12*, 14
pepper(corn)(s):
Cacio e Pepe, *136*, 137
freshly cracked, 19, 38
grinding, 19
seasoning to taste with, 39
Steak, Simple, *88*, 89
pepper mills, *13*, 15, 19
peppers, bell, 229
persimmons, 229
Pesto Pasta, *140*, 141
pilafs:
Brown Rice, *178*, 179
Sweet Pea Bulgur Wheat, *180*,
181
pineapple, 229

pine nut(s):
Butter Lettuce Salad with Parsley &, *194*, 195
Toasted, & Cranberry Quinoa,
*182*, 183
toasting, 37
Pita Pizza, Tuna & Apple, 227,
*227*
pizza:
Margherita, *142*, 143
Tuna & Apple Pita, 227, *227*
plums, 229
pomegranate(s), 229
Seeds, Cottage Cheese &, 220,
*220*
pork:
Chops, Apple Cider, *102*, 103
internal temperature & doneness of, 231
Loin with Apples & Onions,
*100*, 101
patting dry before cooking, 43
storage guideline for, 232
portobello mushrooms:
buying & storing, 165
Roasted Lemon-Thyme, *164*,
165
potatoes, 229
buying & storing, 153
Fries, Oven, *162*, 163
Herb-Roasted Beef with Carrots &, *90*, 91
new, 229
Red, Smashed, with Chives,
*152*, 153
Skillet-Roasted Chicken &,
*68*, 69
pot holders, *13*, 15
pots, *8*, 9
poultry:
internal temperature & doneness of, 231
storage guidelines for, 232
Turkey Bolognese, *128*, 129
see also chicken

produce, washing, 43
Prosciutto, Pear, & Parmesan,
226, *226*

**Q**

quickies, 219–27
    *see also* breakfast quickies;
        lunch or dinner quickies
Quinoa, Toasted Pine Nut & Cran-
    berry, *182*, 183

**R**

radishes, 229
raisin(s):
    Chocolate Chia Drops, *208*,
        209
    Golden, Broccoli with Garlic &,
        *146*, 147
    Oatmeal, & Maple Cookies,
        *206*, 207
Red Potatoes, Smashed, with
    Chives, *152*, 153
refried beans, in Huevos Ranche-
    ros, *54*, 55
refrigerator, how to store in, 233
rhubarb, 229
rice:
    brown, cooking, 189
    Brown, Pilaf, *178*, 179
    Cake with Cucumbers & Salsa,
        224, *224*
    Chicken with Peas &, *70*, 71
    crispy brown rice cereal, in
        Drops (Chocolate Chia
        Drops, Peanut Butter Drops,
        & Cherry-Ginger-Almond
        Drops), *208*, 209
    Stir-fried, with Sunny-side Up
        Eggs, *188*, 189
ricotta:
    Lemon Pancakes, *58*, 59
    Slow-Cooker Lasagna, *134*, 135
    & Tomato on Toast, 223, *223*
roast(ed):
    Asparagus with Lemon, *154*, 155

Beef, Herb-Roasted, with Pota-
    toes & Carrots, *90*, 91
Brussels Sprouts, *160*, 161
Cauliflower & Sage, *158*, 159
Chicken, Seriously Basic, *84*,
    85
Chicken, Sweet Potatoes, &
    Tomatoes, *78*, 79
Chicken Drumsticks–4 Easy
    Recipes! (Barbecue
    Chicken, Mustard & Rose-
    mary Chicken, Yogurt &
    Cumin Chicken, Lemon &
    Sage Chicken), *82*, 83
Chicken Wings, Sweet &
    Spicy, *80*, 81
Eggplant & Cherry Tomatoes,
    *156*, 157
Portobello Mushrooms, Lemon-
    Thyme, *164*, 165
Striped Bass & Tomatoes, *108*,
    109
Sweet Potato Coins, *166*, 167
*see also* skillet-roasted
rosemary, 32
    Chicken Under a "Brick," *72*,
        73
    & Garlic Cannellini Beans, *186*,
        187
    & Mustard Chicken, *82*, 83

**S**

sage, 32
    & Lemon Chicken, *82*, 83
    Roasted Cauliflower &, *158*,
        159
salads, 191–201
    Arugula, Dates, Blue Cheese,
        & Almonds, 225, *225*
    Butter Lettuce, with Pine Nuts
        & Parsley, *194*, 195
    Chicken, with Apples & Basil,
        *200*, 201
    Couscous, with Chickpeas,
        Tomatoes, & Mint, *184*, 185

Kale,–3 Easy Recipes!
    (Toasted Sesame Seed
    Vinaigrette, Honey-Shallot
    Vinaigrette, & Caesar Vin-
    aigrette), *192*, 193
Spinach, Warm, with Blue
    Cheese, *196*, 197
Tomato & Watermelon, with
    Toasted Almonds, *198*, 199
salad spinners, *13*, 15
    washing greens in, 43
salmon:
    cooking with skin on, 41
    Succulent Lemon-Thyme, *110*,
        111
Salsa, 93*f*
    Huevos Rancheros, *54*, 55
    Rice Cake with Cucumbers &,
        224, *224*
salt, seasoning with, 39
sandwiches:
    Apple-Cheddar Melt, 225,
        *225*
    Hamburger, the Most Simple,
        Broiled, Perfect, *94*, 95
    Sliced Tomato & Egg Open-
        Faced, 227, *227*
Sautéed Spinach & Garlic, *150*,
    151
scallions, prepping & slicing, 31
seafood, *see* fish & seafood
seasonality, 229
seasoning to taste, 39
Sesame Seed, Toasted, Vinai-
    grette, 193
set up, *20*, 21
shallot(s), 229
    Honey Vinaigrette, 193*f*
    slicing or chopping, 30
Shepherd's French Toast, *56*, 57
shrimp:
    Crispy, *118*, 119
    peeling & deveining, 40
    Stewy, with Tomatoes & White
        Beans, *120*, 121

sides:
Asparagus, Roasted, with Lemon, *154*, 155
Broccoli with Golden Raisins & Garlic, *146*, 147
Brown Rice Pilaf, *178*, 179
Brussels Sprouts, Roasted, *160*, 161
Bulgur Wheat Pilaf, Sweet Pea, *180*, 181
Butter Lettuce Salad with Pine Nuts & Parsley, *194*, 195
Cannellini Beans, Garlic & Rosemary, *186*, 187
Cauliflower, Roasted, & Sage, *158*, 159
Corn, Mexican, *172*, 173
Couscous Salad with Chickpeas, Tomatoes, & Mint, *184*, 185
Eggplant & Cherry Tomatoes, Roasted, *156*, 157
Fries, Oven (Carrot Fries, Parsnip Fries, & Russet Potato Fries), *162*, 163
Green Beans with Almonds, *148*, 149
Kale Chips, *174*, 175
Kale Salads—3 Easy Recipes! (Toasted Sesame Seed Vinaigrette, Honey-Shallot Vinaigrette, & Caesar Vinaigrette), *192*, 193
Portobello Mushrooms, Roasted Lemon-Thyme, *164*, 165
Quinoa, Toasted Pine Nut & Cranberry, *182*, 183
Red Potatoes, Smashed, with Chives, *152*, 153
Spinach, Sautéed, & Garlic, *150*, 151
Spinach Salad, Warm, with Blue Cheese, *196*, 197
Sugar Snaps, Minty, *168*, 169

Sweet Potato Coins, Roasted, *166*, 167
Tomato & Watermelon Salad with Toasted Almonds, *198*, 199
Tomato Bruschetta, Summer, *170*, 171
skillet-roasted:
Potatoes & Chicken, *68*, 69
Rosemary Chicken Under a "Brick," *72*, 73
skillets, 8, 9
Skirt Steak, Chili-Rubbed, Tacos (with Salsa & Guacamole), *92*, 93
Slow-Cooker Lasagna, *134*, 135
slow cookers, 17
Smashed Red Potatoes with Chives, *152*, 153
Smoothie, Blueberry-Almond, 223, *223*
Soft-boiled Eggs with Toast a.k.a. The Granny Egg, *50*, 51
Spaghetti Marinara, *132*, 133
spatulas:
metal, *12*, 15
silicone, *13*, 15
spices, 19
spinach, 229
buying & storing, 151
Halibut over, Perfect, *114*, 115
Salad, Warm, with Blue Cheese, *196*, 197
Sautéed, & Garlic, *150*, 151
Slow-Cooker Lasagna, *134*, 135
Stir-fried Rice with Sunny-side Up Eggs, *188*, 189
washing, 43
spoons, wooden or bamboo spoons, *13*, 15
springform pans, *11*, 15
steak:
Chili-Rubbed Skirt, Tacos (with Salsa & Guacamole), *92*, 93
Peppercorn, Simple, *88*, 89

Stewy Shrimp with Tomatoes & White Beans, *120*, 121
Stir-fried Rice with Sunny-side Up Eggs, *188*, 189
storage guidelines, 232–33
strainers, *10*, 14
strawberries, 229
Marinated, with Ice Cream, *214*, 215
with Yogurt & Balsamic, 221, *221*
Striped Bass & Tomatoes, Roasted, *108*, 109
sugar snap peas, 229
buying & storing, 169
Minty, *168*, 169
Summer Tomato Bruschetta, *170*, 171
Sweet & Spicy Chicken Wings, *80*, 81
sweet potato(es), 229
buying & storing, 167
Coins, Roasted, *166*, 167
Roasted Chicken, Tomatoes &, *78*, 79

**T**
Tacos, Chili-Rubbed Skirt Steak (with Salsa & Guacamole), *92*, 93
Tex-Mex & Mexican cooking:
Chili, Your First, *96*, 97
Chili-Rubbed Skirt Steak Tacos (with Salsa & Guacamole), *92*, 93
Huevos Rancheros, *54*, 55
Mexican Corn, *172*, 173
thawing foods, 233
thermometers, *12*, 14–15
thyme, 32
Lemon Roasted Portobello Mushrooms, *164*, 165
Lemon Salmon, Succulent, *110*, 111
timers, *12*, 15

toast:
    Avocado, 222, *222*
    Bruschetta, Summer Tomato, *170*, 171
    Tomato & Ricotta on, 223, *223*
toasters, *17*
tomato(es), 229
    Broiled, Fried Eggs over, *48*, 49
    Bruschetta, Summer, *170*, 171
    buying & storing, 171
    Cherry, Roasted Eggplant &, *156*, 157
    Couscous Salad with Chickpeas, Mint &, *184*, 185
    Garlic & Rosemary Cannellini Beans, *186*, 187
    & Ricotta on Toast, 223, *223*
    Roasted Chicken, Sweet Potatoes &, *78*, 79
    Roasted Striped Bass &, *108*, 109
    Salsa, 93*f*
    Sliced, & Egg Open-Faced Sandwich, 227, *227*
    Slow-Cooker Lasagna, *134*, 135
    Spaghetti Marinara, *132*, 133
    Stewy Shrimp with White Beans &, *120*, 121
    Sweet Cherry, Pasta, *124*, 125
    Turkey Bolognese, *128*, 129
    & Watermelon Salad with Toasted Almonds, *198*, 199
tongs, *12*, 14
tortillas, corn:
    Chili-Rubbed Skirt Steak Tacos (with Salsa & Guacamole), *92*, 93
    Huevos Rancheros, *54*, 55
    Tuna & Apple Pita Pizza, 227, *227*

Turkey Bolognese, *128*, 129
turnips, 229

**V**
vegetables, 145–75
    Asparagus, Roasted, with Lemon, *154*, 155
    Broccoli with Golden Raisins & Garlic, *146*, 147
    Brussels Sprouts, Roasted, *160*, 161
    Cauliflower, Roasted, & Sage, *158*, 159
    Corn, Mexican, *172*, 173
    Eggplant & Cherry Tomatoes, Roasted, *156*, 157
    Fries, Oven (Carrot Fries, Parsnip Fries, & Russet Potato Fries), *162*, 163
    Green Beans with Almonds, *148*, 149
    Kale Chips, *174*, 175
    Portobello Mushrooms, Roasted Lemon-Thyme, *164*, 165
    Red Potatoes, Smashed, with Chives, *152*, 153
    Spinach, Sautéed, & Garlic, *150*, 151
    Sugar Snaps, Minty, *168*, 169
    Sweet Potato Coins, Roasted, *166*, 167
    Tomato Bruschetta, Summer, *170*, 171
    washing, 43
vegetarian meals:
    Cacio e Pepe, *136*, 137
    Cannellini Beans, Garlic & Rosemary, *186*, 187
    Egg Noodles & Cheese, Baked, *130*, 131
    Freaky Greek Pasta, *126*, 127

Lasagna, Slow-Cooker, *134*, 135
Pesto Pasta, *140*, 141
Quinoa, Toased Pine Nut & Cranberry, *182*, 183
Roasted Eggplant & Cherry Tomatoes, *156*, 157
Spaghetti Marinara, *132*, 133
Sweet Cherry Tomato Pasta, *124*, 125
vinaigrettes:
    Caesar, 193*f*
    Honey-Shallot, 193*f*
    Red Wine, 195
    Toasted Sesame Seed, 193

**W**
walnuts, in Broiled Honey-Nut Bananas, *212*, 213
Warm Spinach Salad with Blue Cheese, *196*, 197
Wasa with Cottage Cheese & Pomegranate Seeds, 220, *220*
Watermelon & Tomato Salad with Toasted Almonds, *198*, 199
Whipped Cream, 211
whisks, *12*, 15
White Beans, Stewy Shrimp with Tomatoes, *120*, 121
wine openers, *12*, 14
wire cooling racks, *11*, 15
wooden or bamboo spoons, *13*, 15

**Y**
yogurt:
    Blueberry-Almond Smoothie, 223, *223*
    & Cumin Chicken, *82*, 83
    Strawberries with Balsamic &, 221, *221*

**Z**
zucchini, 229

# Special thanks to:

Sara Quessenberry, who I can never, ever,
thank enough for being the best partner in crime.

Jennifer Rudolph Walsh at WME for everything.

Greer Hendricks, Judith Curr, and the Atria team
for making this book a pleasure every step of the way.

Mara Buxbaum, Tara, Rhett, Alla, and Kendall at ID-PR.
And Tom Keaney, always.

The creative team on this book: John Kernick (photography),
Pam Morris (styling), Amy Harte and Merideth Harte, 3&Co. (book design),
Michelle Blakely (wine support and comedic inspiration).
The exceptional Mark Seliger (cover photography) with
special mention to Ruth Levy.

Ricardo Souza, for being the other wonderful man
I look forward to seeing every day.

*Thanks also to **Splendid** and **Gracious Home**.

NOW, WASN'T THAT FUN?